The
Bold
Testament

BEGINNER'S GUIDE TO THE HEBREW BIBLE

Volume I:
Interpretive & Theological Approach

Jonathan M. McCarty

Copyright © 2025
All Rights Reserved

ISBN: 978-1-967441-72-3

Dedication

This book is dedicated to the God of gods: YHWH, the Holy One of Israel. He is my King, Lord, & Liberator: Yeshua of Nazareth, YHWH's Eternal Messiah, Who is the Word of YHWH become flesh. He is the Breath Who makes me holy. He is my Beloved. I am His, and He is mine. His provision made this possible.

Jealous God

On the back cover of this book, you'll find this picture. So, what's with the bird? The Bible tells us that our Creator is a *"jealous God."* It even goes so far as to say that **"Jealous"** is one of His Names:

"You shall not worship any other god,
for YaHWeH, Whose Name is **Jealous**, is a *jealous God*."
Exodus 34:14

Yet the Bible also tells us that **God is Love** and **Love is <u>not</u> jealous** (see 1 John 4:8-16 & 1 Corinthians 13:4). The answer to this apparent contradiction rests in the original languages beyond the English text we read. In Hebrew, the root behind the word that our English translates as **"jealous"** means **"bird's nest."** The idea is the passionate protection a mother bird has toward her nest. Likewise, God—as our Father—is **"jealous"** (**passionately protective**) for us, constantly watching us and guarding us from any predator who would try to harm us. In the Bible's story, all other so-called "gods" are predators that ultimately just want to steal us from our nest and eat us up.

In this, we see that God's "jealousy" is not based on selfishness or insecurity. His "jealousy" is His commitment to protect His nest from every threat at all costs — even if it costs Him His Life. With that in mind, I encourage you to look up the song "**How He Loves / Jealous**" by UPPERROOM & Elyssa Smith. You can find the song on YouTube at the link below:

https://www.youtube.com/watch?v=6dh0SPupoUI

Close your eyes, listen to the words, and trust that you have a Father Who loves you exactly like this. He is *for you*, for your protection and your freedom. He will forever stand against everything that would seek to hurt you or make you a slave.

Acknowledgments

I want to thank my dad, Michael McCarty, for always believing in me and encouraging me to do what God made me to do. Without his trust in Jesus, this book would not exist. Even more, my dad inspired me to seek Truth over tradition and to love God with all my heart, soul, mind, and strength.

About the Author

Jonathan McCarty has been a devoted disciple of Jesus Christ since he was 3 years old. He is a Bible teacher & writer with 13 years of experience in the field of Biblical Studies. Though he grew up in church and spent 7 years serving at his church as a youthleader, he began seeking to know the original context of the Bible outside his culture & theological background when he was 17 years old. Jonathan prioritizes Truth over tradition. Though he is a Gentile, he has a passion for Jewish history and culture. One of his most important goals is to explain the Bible in its original historical, cultural, & linguistic context. In his study of the Bible and all other subjects, Jonathan seeks to grow his personal faith and sees atheist perspectives as a welcome challenge in this process.

Table of Contents

INTRODUCTION

What Is the Hebrew Bible? Why Learn About It? 11
What to Expect from This Series 18

VOLUME I

Chapter 1:
Introduction to Worldview

Seeing through Your Glasses 22
From Paganism to the Catholic Church 25
From the Catholic Church to Humanism 28

Chapter 2:
Humanism: The Dominant Modern Worldview

From Reason to Realism 31
From Realism to Postmodernism 32
Postmodernism Vs. Modernism 34

Chapter 3:
Naturalism's Role in Modern Biblical Interpretation

The Worldview of Naturalism 36
A Godless Universe 38
Source & Form Criticism 39
Authors J, E, D, and P in the Documentary Hypothesis 54

The Yahwist (J) 55

The Elohimist (E) 56

The Deuteronomist (D) 58

The Priestly Writer (P) and Other Editors (R) 59

The Origin of Ancient Israel & Their Pagan Practices 63

The Origin of Monotheism 72

The Canaanite Connection 74

The Mystery of YHWH 78

Israelite Henotheism Affirming Naturalist Worldview 91

The Mythicist Vs. Historicist Perspectives on the Bible 92

Archaeology's Importance in Studying the Bible 95

Chapter 4:
The Worldview of Judaism

Five Types of Judaism 98

The Legacy of Rabbinic Judaism 100

Sola Scriptura Jews 100

Jewish Responses to Jesus 102

Rabbinic Judaism Vs. The Israelite Religion 104

The Bible (TaNaK) in the Worldview of Judaism 105

The Supremacy of the Torah 107

Chapter 5:
The Worldview of Christianity

The Old Testament in the Worldview of Christianity 109

Why Christians Haven't Rejected the Old Testament 111

God's Word: A Lesser Revelation? *112*
Old Testament Interpretations in Christianity *113*

Chapter 6:
How Other Worldviews Read the Bible

The Bible in the Worldview of Blended Beliefs *116*
My Approach in This Series *119*

Image References **123**

Introduction

What Is the Hebrew Bible? Why Learn About It?

The best-selling and most influential book in the world today is the Christian Bible. While Christians tend to value the New Testament more than the Old Testament, it is undeniable that the New Testament would not exist without the Old Testament. The Old Testament is the first part of the Christian Bible, and it is the foundation of the New Testament. The Old Testament tells the story of the Hebrew people, and it was originally written in the ancient Hebrew language. For this reason, it is more accurate to refer to the writings of the Old Testament as the Hebrew Bible. This book is the first volume of a 3-part series that will give you a thorough guide to the Hebrew Bible. This first volume focuses on the subject of worldview.

This series is for everyone who wants to learn more about what I would argue is the most important piece of literature in the modern world. Some today would argue that the Old Testament is an outdated religious text which is unworthy of any academic research. Even the name which Western society has given this text—the "<u>Old</u>" Testament—indicates our general attitude toward it. But others recognize that the world today would not be what it is without the Hebrew Bible.

Based on these observations, I begin by asking you this key question: Why should we study a religious text, especially a religious text that is as "outdated" as the Old Testament? Consider the religions of the world today based on our current population of just under 8 billion people around the globe. This chart shows the worldwide popularity of each religious affiliation based on percentage:

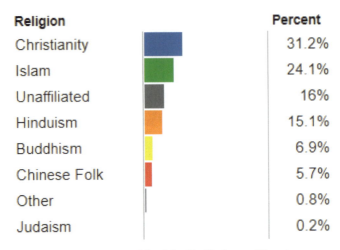

Religion	Percent
Christianity	31.2%
Islam	24.1%
Unaffiliated	16%
Hinduism	15.1%
Buddhism	6.9%
Chinese Folk	5.7%
Other	0.8%
Judaism	0.2%

Image 1: Worldwide Religions Chart

The third most popular religion in the world today is no religion at all. However, even without religion, most people today would agree with the basic principles of human rights. Human rights are one of the key cornerstones of modern politics in the Western world. The concept of human rights is ultimately a religious idea. We accept that all people have inborn rights simply because we choose to believe it. The idea that all individuals and groups of people have inborn rights and value in their existence is ultimately derived from the 3 major Abrahamic religions of the world today: **Christianity**, **Islam**, and **Judaism**. For those who have no religion, studying these Abrahamic religions will help develop their understanding of the origin of human rights.

Studying religions gives us insight into the value systems of our ancestors and the other ancient people of this world. Based on the research of many modern scholars, the history of religion around the world can be traced back to the ideas of **polytheism**: *the belief in many gods which each had their own limited roles in the universe.* Each culture and nation in the ancient world had their own type of polytheism. Polytheism is generally rare today, particularly in Western cultures. The polytheism in India is what ultimately led to the foundation of the religion of **Hinduism**.

Hinduism is now the fourth most popular religion of the world today. The man who has now come to be known as Buddha was born in a background of Hinduism. **Buddhism** arose out of a Hindu culture. Many people today find more value from these far eastern religions than they do from the more popular Western religions. Since the Hebrew Bible presumably has no connection with Hinduism or Buddhism (except for a *shared origin of polytheism*), some may say this is why it is a waste of time to learn the Old Testament.

In this case, I once again point to the fact that the Hebrew Bible is one of the most important pieces of literature to study in connection with the Western origin of **human rights**. The concept that every person on this planet has inherent value and "inalienable" rights does not come from far eastern religions. While these far eastern religions may blend better with **naturalism** (a crucial worldview leading to many modern scientific discoveries), they did little if anything to help develop human rights. On the other hand, the more recently developed worldview of naturalism (without a comprehensive embrace of human rights) led to the beliefs of **Social Darwinism**. Social Darwinism is directly responsible for the atrocities of Adolf Hitler and Nazi Germany. **This is what happens when a worldview focuses more on nature than human beings.**

I would argue that the greatest and most prosperous nations in the world today are those nations that embrace a Western culture that includes a foundational worldview revolving around human rights. The Enlightenment philosophers who imagined the concept of human rights came from the history of this Western culture. The Old Testament played an indispensable role in this history. So, if you believe that all human beings have "inalienable" rights and inherent worth, you should know the origin of this concept in ancient history. This is found in the Hebrew Bible.

Without the Hebrew Bible, the 3 Abrahamic religions we have today would not exist. The polytheism of the ancient Western world gave rise to the 3 major Abrahamic religions of the world today. **Jews**, **Christians**, and **Muslims** all claim that a man named **Abraham** was one of the chief founding fathers of their distinct versions of *faith in only one God*. Both Jews and Muslims claim direct bloodline descent tracing back to Abraham. But Christians see Abraham as a spiritual father of their faith whose ethnicity was less important than his belief.

The second most popular religion in the world today is **Islam**, and some researchers estimate that this religion will become the most popular religion in the world within the next hundred years. At the current time, around 2 billion people—which is about ¼ of the *entire* world population—claim to be Muslims and practice some form of this religion. But what are the origins of Islam?

Muslims believe that Islam is the true faith in Abraham's God that goes all the way back to the creation of the world. But they also believe that the **Prophet Muhammad** was the man who God chose to reveal this faith in its true form after it had become corrupted. Muhammad wrote the Quran, the sacred text of Islam, in the early 600s CE. This was around 600 years after the time of **Jesus Christ**. Muhammad wrote this text after he had an encounter with an angel. Muhammad claimed that this angel was Gabriel from the famous

Christian and Jewish traditions which had developed by that time.

Regardless of whether Muhammad's testimony is true, there are 3 early Muslim historians who wrote accounts about Muhammad's life. These accounts go along with other ancient sources to tell the story of how **Muhammad met a Christian monk** who goes by 3 different names. His Arabic name is Bahira, but his Latin names are Sergius and Nestorius. This Christian monk had a crucial influence in Muhammad's early life. Bahira came from the **heretical Christian tradition of Arianism**—a branch of Christianity that was rejected by most churches. This branch of Christianity **believed that Jesus was only human** and that He was *not* God in the flesh. Bahira's influence in Muhammad's young life strongly suggests that the religion of Islam derived directly from **Christianity**.

Of the 8 billion people in the modern world, **2½ billion people** *claim* **to be Christians.** *This makes Christianity the largest religion in the world today.* Christianity began as an ancient **Jewish cult** revolving around a man whose Hebrew name was Yehoshua (or Yeshua). Through the translation of Hebrew to Greek and then Greek to English, this name in modern English is Jesus. Jesus was a Jewish man from the town of Nazareth in Galilee from the first century CE. He did not originally have a wide following among any people outside of the Jewish community in ancient Israel. The Jews that followed His teachings came to be known as **Nazarenes**.

In a short period of time, this sect of Nazarenes became very popular. The Jews who followed this sect began to bring many non-Jews into it over the course of many years. The center of this sect was originally in **Jerusalem**, but persecution caused this sect to grow and move from Jerusalem to **Antioch**. It was in ancient Antioch where these Nazarenes were first called **Christians**. Christianity began leaning more into a **Greek culture** that was more widely accepted by non-Jews.

In time, the Christians moved their primary leadership from Antioch to **Rome**. This city was the capital of the Roman Empire, the greatest government and political system in the world at that time. At first, Christianity was *illegal* in Rome. The Romans considered Christianity to be a dangerous cult. They persecuted the Christians and tried to kill them all. Despite this, the number of Christians in Rome grew exponentially to the point in which their population outnumbered the polytheistic Roman religion.

Within the 300s CE, Christianity was legalized and then adopted as the *only* official religion of the Roman Empire before 400 CE. It was from that place that **Christianity rapidly came to *dominate* the Western world**. After the fall of the Roman Empire in the west, the political powers of Europe shifted from generation to generation. But in each new political shift, Christianity triumphed over the more ancient European religions that had embraced polytheism. The Christians originally shared the same sacred text as the ancient Jews. But in a short time, they wrote their own additional sacred writings which were eventually collected and put together to form the New Testament.

From these things, we can see clearly that Islam derived from Christianity, and Christianity derived from the same ancient sources that form the roots of modern **Judaism**. The religion of Judaism is unusual in the sense that it is more connected with a specific group of people than with a system of beliefs. Modern Judaism—like all modern religions—comes to us in many different forms. But ultimately, the religion of Judaism is one of the smallest religions in the modern world. Only around 15 million people claim to be Jews— representing only 0.2% of the world population. But despite these smaller numbers, scholars today recognize that the 2 major religions of *both* Christianity and Islam ultimately find their origin in the traditions and stories of **ancient Judaism**. While the major sources for understanding modern Judaism come to us from the Talmud, the Talmud is essentially a commentary on the series of books which form **the Hebrew Bible**.

The Hebrew Bible tells the story of an ancient group of nomads who came to be known as **Hebrews** or **Israelites**. The Hebrews wandered around the ancient world and eventually settled in the territory that came to be called the land of **Canaan**. When the Israelites took political control of this territory, it came to be known as the land of **Israel**. This territory of Israel became a United Kingdom under a man named King David, and it reached its peak of prosperity under the reign of David's son, King Solomon.

But after King Solomon died, some of his servants rebelled against his son and established a separate monarchy in the northern part of the land of Israel. From that point forward, the Northern Kingdom in the land became known as **Israel**, but the **Southern Kingdom** in the land became known as **Judah**. In the course of time, the entire land of Israel was conquered by other nations beginning with the Babylonians. The Babylonians forced most of the people from Judah to relocate to foreign lands. As a result, the people of Judah came to be called **Jews**.

Under the Persian King Cyrus, the Jews were allowed to return to their former homeland and rebuild it. They were allowed to live independently in their homeland again for several hundred years until the Roman Empire conquered their territory shortly before the time of Jesus Christ. Shortly after Jesus' time, the Romans forced the Jews out of their homeland and scattered them all over the world. As a result, the Jews gradually came to identify with other countries in the centuries that followed. But many of them still kept their cultural heritage and traditions throughout the ages.

The land formerly known as Canaan and Israel was renamed **Palestine** by the Roman Empire. This is the ancient history of the Jewish people and religion, and it begins with the Hebrew Bible. The Hebrew Bible contains the oldest written account of the man called **Abraham**. Abraham's supposed **monotheism** forms the basis for the 2 most popular religions in the world today.

For all these reasons, the Hebrew Bible has become the most ancient influential text on the politically dominant Western culture. In the Hebrew Bible, we can see some of the earliest ideas that form the basis for our belief in human rights, we can find the roots of 3 major world religions, and we can gain a clear view into the polytheistic cultures of the ancient world. This is why we should study the Hebrew Bible. Its writings are perhaps more useful for us today than they ever have been before. But we must learn to understand them in their context and in the broader context of ancient Near Eastern history.

What to Expect from This Series

This series will provide a **bird's-eye view of the Hebrew Bible** from *several different angles*. In this series, you will find 3 separate volumes with unique content revolving around the Hebrew Bible. In this first volume, we will discuss the subject of worldview and compare several diverse perspectives which are used to understand the Hebrew Bible. In the second volume, we will explore the historical background, culture, composition, language, and themes of the Hebrew Bible. In the third and final volume, I will present the Hebrew Bible's narrative using a comprehensive outline and chronological timeline.

This series will cover a broad spectrum of subjects connected with the Hebrew Bible. This will include studies in various worldviews, ancient history, archaeology, spoken and written language, Bible translation, the entire Bible's story, interpretive theories, and Messianic prophecies. In this series, you will gain a thorough and clear comprehension of the Old Testament. By reading this series, you will learn to see the New Testament in the "Old" Testament. Finally, you will understand why it is more respectful and accurate to call it the Hebrew Bible.

I will close this introduction with a message to all the Christians who will read this series. I grew up in a Christian household, and throughout my life I have been surrounded by church culture. For that reason, I have seen how many Christians have failed to value the Hebrew Bible. But in the past 12 years I've spent studying this book, I have come to see its critical importance in ways that I never saw or heard about in church. Paul said it best in the New Testament when he wrote to Timothy with these words:

> "**All Scripture** is God-breathed and is useful for teaching, convincing, correcting and training in righteousness, so the man of God may be complete, perfected to *all good works*."

In the original context of this passage, the *Scripture* that Paul was referring to was *the Hebrew Bible*. God does not want us to view any part of the Bible as expired or useless. Everything in it has a significant purpose for our faith today. We should not treat the first part of the Bible as less important. It seems to me that the reason some Christians treat the Old Testament as less important is because they have trouble understanding it compared to our modern traditions and the writings in the New Testament.

Everything that the writers of the New Testament wrote was directly inspired by both their experience with Jesus and their understanding of the Hebrew Bible in light of what they saw from Him. So, we ought to be diligent students of the Hebrew Bible. We should study this "Old" Testament with the same passion that we would study the New Testament. I invite you to engage in this fascinating text with me and come into a deeper relationship with Jesus through it.

Volume I

Interpretive & Theological Approach

Chapter 1

Introduction to Worldview

Seeing through Your Glasses

In this volume we will consider the subject of interpretive and theological approach to the Hebrew Bible. This will cover the most fundamental question of biblical studies: worldview. We will examine different ways that people today view the Bible. Then, we will use this to inform the rest of our study of the text.

There are countless perspectives on the nature of reality and meaning of life, and we cannot cover them all here. But this volume will provide an overview of 5 main worldviews that are typically used to read and understand the Hebrew Bible. First, we will examine two atheistic worldviews typically used to teach about the Hebrew Bible at public schools and universities. We will discuss how these views developed in history. I refer to these 2 views as the Mythicist and Historicist perspectives. These worldviews have some overlap with the others. Next, I will discuss how this text is understood in Judaism, Christianity, and in Blended Beliefs. Finally, I will briefly describe my approach to the Bible.

Like many of you who are reading this, I grew up in a religious household. But regardless of our background, it is important to remember that the third most popular religion in the world today is no religion at all. Western culture has come to form their views based on a dichotomy that has been created between science and religion. On this basis, the American government and others have developed strict policies that advocate for the separation of Church and State. There is a good reason for this that I would elucidate further if this was a history class. But for now, you should be aware of the modern value systems of Western culture that are used to interpret the Bible.

If you are reading this series, I want you to know that I did my best to keep you in mind no matter who you are. I hope that some of you reading this will be non-religious or atheists. I also hope that some of you reading this come from a faith outside of Judaism or Christianity. And of course, I hope that many Jews and Christians will read this series. But no matter who you are, I want you to know that I designed the content of this series for all people.

I include multiple perspectives on the Hebrew Bible here—even the atheistic perspectives on the Bible. This series is useful for everyone who is interested in knowing more about the Old Testament. The Bible is the essential text behind the evolution of the concept of human rights. In this sense, we can learn from the Bible even if we do not embrace any religion that cherishes it as sacred literature.

Image 2: Seeing Clearly through Glasses

Image 3: My Glasses

As you can see in the above photo, I am wearing this pair of glasses because it provides me with a clear vision of the world around me. Without these glasses, things become blurry for me. But these glasses bring everything into focus. They give meaning to the many details that surround my eyes. In the same way, a worldview can be compared to a pair of glasses. Our worldview is what we put on every day and use to bring the rest of our experiences into focus. Before we can study the Bible, we have to decide how we will view it.

Your worldview is what you use to answer the biggest questions about life. These questions include deep philosophical ideas such as "Is there a God?" or "Do human beings have souls?" Your worldview also describes your definition of reality. It is how you answer the question: "What is truth?" Worldview is not the same thing as religion. Your worldview will impact your religion, but it will also impact your political views. For example, there are about two and a half billion Christians in the world today. But these Christians all have different worldviews, especially when it comes to the subject of politics. Some Christians prefer more conservative political principles, and other Christians prefer liberal political theories. Worldview is much deeper than religion.

In the next two sections of this chapter, I will discuss a brief history containing the evolution of the main worldview of Western culture. I will trace this shifting worldview from ancient times up until this present day. We will see how modern education institutions came to develop the dichotomy between science and religion. We will also see how humanism became the most significant value of today's world in both religion and politics. Then, we will discuss the five aspects of humanism from the eras of the Enlightenment to Postmodernism. Finally, we will take a look at how these things relate to the Postmodern Cycle Political Theory.

From Paganism to the Catholic Church

The Western value system of the modern world is rooted in the philosophy of naturalism. To understand how the idea of naturalism developed, we must trace the former worldviews of Western culture from their ancient origins. As I mentioned in the introduction of this book, polytheism (or paganism) was originally the dominant religion of the whole world. The idea of monotheism or belief in one god was ridiculous to most people. Most developed civilizations accepted the idea that many gods competed with each other to rule the universe. This was not just one interpretation of reality in ancient times, but it was basically the only interpretation of reality.

Life was a war between the gods, and people were just slaves caught in the middle of it. Your social status in ancient times determined how the gods viewed you according to their ranks. This mainstream worldview of paganism continued into the time of the Roman Empire. Many historians consider the time of the Roman Empire to be the peak of ancient civilization.

Through the monotheistic and marginal religion of ancient Judaism, Christianity emerged as a prominent new religion in the ancient world. Christianity's popularity grew alongside the powerful Roman Empire. Christianity was illegal in the Roman Empire for a few centuries, and the earliest Christians were terribly persecuted for their faith. The penalty for being a Christian was often being eaten alive by wild beasts or burned alive at circus events. These circus events were a form of public entertainment for Roman citizens. They came to a coliseum to be entertained by various forms of violent slaughter.

This all changed in the early fourth century CE when the Roman Emperor Constantine legalized Christianity. Constantine took many steps to unify and restore the divided Roman Empire of the early fourth century. One of these steps was to legalize Christianity. Following the legalization of Christianity, Constantine helped Christian leaders of that time to standardize their religion into specific doctrines of orthodox faith. This happened at the Council of Nicaea in 325 CE, and this is when the Christian Bible was established as it is today.

The Council of Nicaea is, in many ways, the birthplace of the Holy Roman Catholic Church. The office of the pope in the Catholic Church was originally the position of the bishop of Rome. There were many Christian bishops in many different ancient cities by that time, but the city of Rome had become the most important. Rome became the center of Christianity by the fourth century. Some Protestants view Constantine as the man who acted as the first Pope. Others view him as the one who lifted up the bishop of Rome and made it possible for popes to rule over Europe with supreme political power in the future.

Constantine did much more than help create the Catholic Church. Constantine reunified the Roman Empire after a period of terrible civil wars. As part of this reunification process, Constantine moved Rome's central government to the Eastern side of the Roman Empire. In doing this, Constantine changed the capital of the empire from the city of Rome to the city of Byzantium. It was only around a century and a half later that the Roman Empire fell in the West. This gave rise to the chaotic era of the Dark Ages. The remaining empire in the East became known as the Byzantine Empire.

While Emperor Constantine did legalize Christianity, he did so with a general policy of religious tolerance. He wanted everyone in the empire to have religious freedom. No one had to be a Christian, and many pagans still lived in the empire and practiced their declining faith on a regular basis. Constantine himself was a pagan until much later in his life. But only sixty years after Constantine legalized Christianity, a new Roman Emperor named Theodosius I made Christianity the only legal religion of the Roman Empire.

All paganism and other religions were outlawed. This exponentially increased the power of the Catholic Church. Pagans began to be persecuted for their faith, and every citizen of the Roman Empire was forced to either convert to Christianity or die. Orthodox Christian faith as explained by the Nicaean Creed became the only acceptable religion. All other faiths which diverged from the ideas of the Nicaean Creed began to be branded with the term 'heresy.' All rebels to the orthodox Christian faith became heretics. The penalty for heresy was death.

This type of so-called "Christian" tyranny continued throughout the rest of the Middle Ages. One century after Emperor Theodosius I, the Roman Empire in Western Europe collapsed. This happened because of many different factors which historians are still discussing to this day. The city of Rome was flooded with Germanic tribes from northeastern Europe, and these Germanic tribes began to take over Europe. Consequently, a power vacuum was created in Europe. Chaos reigned as many ancient European tribes competed for power and terrorized the former citizens of the Roman Empire.

While the Germanic tribes gloried in their conquest of Rome, they also carried an obsession with resurrecting the Roman Empire with their own people as its rulers. This obsession with the Roman Empire continued in history and can even be seen in prominent Western symbols such as the German and American Eagle. During this time of great instability, the most stabilizing social network of Western Europe was the Catholic Church. The Catholic Church came to fill the power vacuum left by the fallen Roman Empire in Medieval Times. For a while, the Catholic Church system became the only centralized government in Europe, and one might even say it was the original European Union.

From the Catholic Church to Humanism

While the Germanic tribes conquered all the lands of Europe, the religion of Christianity conquered all the hearts of Europe. This further increased the power of the Catholic Church. All the Germanic tribes eventually abandoned their pagan roots in favor of the Catholic Christian faith. As a result of this and other political factors in this era of history, the Pope (formerly called the bishop of Rome) became the supreme spiritual and political authority in Europe. The Pope had more power than kings and their kingdoms. The Catholic Church's sophisticated network of local churches helped solidify its central power.

At the height of the Catholic Church's reign over Europe, the Church came to see itself as the literal Kingdom of God on Earth. With this view of the world firmly established, the Pope was in place of God Himself. The Church abused their spiritual authority and began using it for political and financial gain. The Catholic Church's leadership became severely corrupt, and people slowly began to question the Church's legitimacy as God's chosen ruler on Earth. This challenge to the Church's authority was solidified by events that took place between the mid-fourteenth and sixteenth centuries.

First, the Black Plague killed one third of the entire European population. During this devastating pandemic, the Catholic Church's theology about punishment for sin was no longer sufficient to explain the horrors of human suffering. The Black Plague led to the further development of humanism in Europe, and it caused people to lose faith in the Catholic Church.

Second, the conquests and discoveries of the European Crusaders led to an influx of wealth and culture in Europe. This combined with other factors to create the period of the Renaissance. The word Renaissance means "rebirth," and it refers to the rebirth of ancient Greek and Roman ideals manifested in literature, art, and other forms of creative thinking. People began to look to nature for answers rather than to imagine an abstract spiritual world. These things slowly led to the birth of naturalist philosophy and the growing popularity of humanism.

Within the last five hundred years, humanism has spread to every area of both community and individual life in the Western world. The events of the Protestant Reformation caused the Christian religion to fragment into thousands of different denominations. Meanwhile, other related political events exposed government corruption at the highest levels. First, the wealthy and powerful people in society became free to challenge the Catholic Church. Second, the common people in society became free to challenge the wealthy and powerful. This led to events such as the American and French Revolutions which established democratic policies as the main form of Western government.

All these events formed the background for the development of five evolving aspects of humanism. These five aspects can be traced in five distinct periods of history: the Enlightenment, Romanticism, Realism, Modernism, and Postmodernism. In the next chapter, we will examine these five eras of recent history and explain how their philosophies interact with each other today.

Chapter 2

Humanism: The Dominant Modern Worldview

From Reason to Realism

Humanism is basically a human-centered view of the world. It views everything else with humanity as the centerpiece. Humanism is the unspoken and unofficial worldview of the modern era. Humanism sees individual or communal human experience as the final authority on the definition of truth. While most of us in the world today are humanists, we all have different views on what being a humanist is all about. We all have different approaches to the truth about our lives and experiences. The key question we all must answer is: What is real, and how do we know for sure?

My argument for this book is that while most of us in the Western world today are humanists, we all disagree about what aspect of our humanism we should emphasize. Based on the events of the past 300 years, there are 5 unique aspects of humanism that have developed. These aspects form the 5 types of humanism. Each type presents a unique answer to that key question: "What is real and how do we know for sure?" Now we will explore these five types of humanism in their respective periods of recent history.

The first period of this history began with the Scientific Revolution in the 1400s. The Scientific Revolution began when Nicholas Copernicus' ideas about the universe were confirmed by the discovery of Galileo and other early scientific minds. Subsequent scientific developments eventually led to the period in history known as the Enlightenment or the Age of Reason. This took place between 1715 and 1800 CE. This period of humanism was marked by an emphasis on rational thinking.

In the Enlightenment perspective, reason is valued above emotion and every other type of search for meaning in life. The generation after the Enlightenment period reacted to intense rationalism by swinging the pendulum to the other side of human experience: emotion. This led to the Romantic Era which was marked by the philosophies of Romanticism. While the Enlightenment emphasized reason, Romanticism emphasizes feelings and emotions. This Romantic Era lasted from 1800 to 1850 CE, and it led to an increased interest in individual experiences above group identities.

Around 1850 CE, the Industrial Revolution took place. This paved the way for rapid technological growth leading up to modern times. People who lived during the Industrial Revolution began to reject both the intense rationalism of the Enlightenment and the intense emotionalism of Romanticism. They developed the humanist philosophy of Realism. Realism focuses on the practical details of objective reality instead of the subjective features of the human mind. Realism emphasizes what is practical for physical production and accomplishment.

From Realism to Postmodernism

The period of Realism led to brutal political policies which eventually led to the horrific events of World War I in the early 20th century. In reaction to the terrible events of that war, the Western world moved toward the humanist philosophy of Modernism. This has been the main philosophy of education institutions in the

Western world for the past hundred years.

While Realism assumes that the truth about life is obvious and unquestionable, Modernism protests to this assertion. Instead, Modernism is the view that truth has to be carefully searched out through a process of diligent research with a community of people. Truth cannot be discovered by any individual human being. It must be reached in connection with community. Modernism glorifies democracy as the ideal form of government. A Modernist would argue that the best way to make a decision for a community is to vote on different options. In Modernism, truth is ultimately determined by majority rule.

The terrible events of World War II demonstrated the failures of both Realism and Modernism. Many people in the West up to this day still embrace Modernism as the best philosophy to determine truth. But others reject it in favor of Postmodernism, a new philosophy which was formed in the 1970s by philosophers such as Jean-Francois Lyotard and Jean Baudrillard. In the years since its origin, many people who studied Postmodernism misunderstood it and thought that it was equivalent to relativism.

Relativism proposes the theory that truth is relative. Relativism proposes that there is no such thing as absolute truth since truth is limited to human experience. Many Christian educators confuse Relativism and Postmodernism because they have not studied Postmodernism in its origins. Postmodernism does not propose that truth does not exist. Instead, Postmodernism believes that truth exists in an inaccessible form. On that basis, truth can never be presented with perfect accuracy. Truth can only be presented as an approximation of its absolute form.

According to Postmodern Theory, truth is not flexible in its existence, but it is flexible in its expression. This understanding of reality has significant practical applications. When considering postmodernism, people and governments are challenged to work hard to continually find new presentations of the truth in this ever-changing world. Truth never changes, but its fullness is unavailable to us except in limited approximations. Truth defies legitimation. This means that truth tends to become twisted when it is conformed to systems of law or rigid government policies used to enforce the law.

In the modern world, the views of Realism, Modernism, and Postmodernism are in continual conflict with each other. Postmodernism says: "The Truth is beyond my personal experience. I will never stop searching for it, but I will never say I have fully attained it." Modernism says: "The Truth is within our grasp! If we work together, we can have it all." Realism says: "I have the Truth, and I am the Truth. If you defy me, you defy both reality and your place in it."

Hopefully it goes without saying that Realism is the most dangerous worldview of these three. Sadly, Realism is also the easiest worldview to accept. Modernism always leads directly to Realism. Postmodernism challenges Realism and brings us to a place of humility.

Postmodernism Vs. Modernism

The modern education systems of today typically reject Postmodernism in favor of Modernism. The grading system and standardized testing systems would not work with a postmodern worldview. For this reason, educators typically take a modernist approach when searching for truth. Furthermore, postmodernism severely lacks political efficiency because it resists being conformed to an agenda. Modernism is able to support a realist agenda and advance it to the stage of full implementation. This happens when the majority of people agree to one particular presentation of truth above all others.

Essentially, Modernism proposes that truth can be perfectly expressed and presented in a certain form if people come together to work hard enough to find it. But Postmodernism rejects this proposal and asserts that pure truth cannot be perfectly presented or expressed except in vague approximations. Postmodernism is the unseen and unpresentable reality in which we live. This reality has allowed local communities of diverse cultures all over the world to thrive since ancient times.

But Postmodernism tends to give birth to Modernism. This happens when a certain community of people decide that their presentation of truth is better than all the others. Modernism then slowly transforms into the hideous monster that is Realism. Practically, this happens when a government enforces one single presentation of truth which deceptively labels all others as 'lies.' Modernism inevitably leads to some form of Realism. In every Realist worldview, everyone assumes that truth is obvious and anyone who resists it should be punished.

This is the Postmodern Cycle Political Theory. It may seem irrelevant in this cursory glance which I am giving you, but this theory is essential for every field of study is modern education systems. There is much more that I could say about these five aspects of humanism and their impact on modern political theories. But for our purposes in this book, I wanted to simply give you an introduction to these things. In the next chapter, we will discuss the worldview of naturalism as it developed in these different eras of humanism.

Chapter 3

Naturalism's Role in Modern Biblical Interpretation

The Worldview of Naturalism

This chapter is essential to understand **how the Bible is understood and taught in public schools and universities today**. So, pay close attention and keep these things in mind as we move forward in this series. Some would argue that the **philosophy of naturalism** goes back to ancient **Indian philosophy**. In this sense, it is connected to Indian religions such as **Hinduism**. But the ideas of naturalism were *mostly* unpopular in the Western world until much later.

One of the greatest products of the Enlightenment's Age of Reason was the Western development of the **worldview of naturalism**. Scientists further solidified the worldview of naturalism in the academic world of modern times. Among the most notable of these scientists is **Charles Darwin**. Darwin's theories about nature led to the discovery and invention of **the theory of biological evolution**.

Naturalism is a type of Realism. Naturalism proposes that the belief in nature is the obvious and most reliable source of truth. Nature refers to the physical, material, and visible world all around us. Naturalism began as a humanist philosophy since people recognized that we are a part of nature and nature is a part of us. But naturalism has transcended humanist philosophy since its origins.

Theism refers to *any* form of belief in a god or gods. Historians today typically refer to the pagan religion of the ancient world as **polytheism:** *the belief in many gods*. This stands in contrast to **monotheism, the belief in *only one* God. Naturalism rejects *all* forms of theism** *except* <u>atheism</u> and <u>pantheism</u>. For this reason, naturalism is generally *associated* with atheism. But it is important to understand the *difference* between atheism and naturalism. There are *many* people who believe in God that are *also* naturalists, but these people typically embrace some form of **pantheism**.

The common theme of naturalism is the **rejection of a supernatural worldview**. In the view of naturalism, everything that people have called a god or gods could be explained as a **phenomenon of nature**. Naturalists do not believe that there is a spiritual world *at all*. They believe that nature is *the only reality* all around us. Nature's complexity is what has led us to think that there is a supernatural world. For this reason, *both* **atheism and pantheism support the view of naturalism**. So, what is the difference between atheism and pantheism?

Atheists believe that **no gods exist** *at all*. In the atheist mindset, everything that *could* be called a god is *actually* just a **projection of human consciousness upon nature**. The only true gods are people who magnify themselves and conceptualize themselves in a grand, cosmic form. An atheist would argue that gods refer to legends and myths about imaginary superhumans who could manipulate nature on a whim.

Pantheism is essentially *the exact opposite* **of atheism**. For this reason, it is *ironic* that pantheism is the only other theism that supports the views of naturalism. While atheism says that there are *no gods*, **pantheism proposes that** <u>*all things*</u> **in nature are God**. In the pantheist mindset, **God and the Universe are synonyms** for each other. Everything that people describe as a miracle could be explained by natural phenomena. All natural phenomena are literally the works of God since God *is* Nature. Pantheists *do not* believe that God *created* nature. Instead, pantheists believe that **God is Nature**.

Pantheism is the unspoken worldview of *many* Eastern and New Age religions in the modern world. These religions focus on the idea of **supreme consciousness**. Pantheism's influence can be seen in Hollywood sitcoms and movies today, such as the popular show *How I Met Your Mother*. In this show and others, the characters in the stories refer to *"The Universe"* as having a purpose and a plan for everyone's life. The Universe is *a synonym for God* because **God is Nature**.

When discussing the subject of worldview, it is important to be aware of the worldviews of pantheism and atheism. We can see how these 2 connect with each other paradoxically. It is my purpose in this book to introduce you to these dual perspectives on naturalism. Not all naturalists are atheists, but popular opinion still associates naturalism with atheism.

A Godless Universe

As I mentioned previously, naturalism is typically associated with atheism and those who reject a supernatural view of the world. With this in mind, we now turn to the main subject of **how the Bible is viewed in naturalist philosophy**. Based on the Western religious traditions associated with Christianity, the **Hebrew Bible** is typically named the *Old Testament*.

Naturalists embrace a scientific and rationalistic perspective on life and history. They *do not believe* in angels *or* demons, and they *do not* believe in miracles in the traditional sense. However, some of them may accept the proposition that a "miracle" is an unusual phenomenon in nature which was celebrated by ancient people as an act of a god *or* the gods.

Remember, not all naturalists are atheists despite the association between these 2 worldviews. **Naturalists hold tightly to a nature-centered view of reality.** In their perspective, *everything* that the Bible describes as an act of God can be explained by natural phenomena. Here are 2 examples of the naturalist worldview of the Bible from the *Book of Exodus*. First, **God parting the Red Sea** is sometimes explained as a time when **the tide was particularly low at a place where it was normally deep.** Second, the story of **God coming down to see the Israelites as a consuming fire at Mount Sinai** is sometimes explained as a **massive volcanic eruption**. But the Israelites thought this was a manifestation of their God.

Naturalists prefer concrete explanations of biblical events which conform to natural phenomena. They resist abstract and supernatural explanations of these events. They refuse to believe *any* interpretation of the Bible that accepts a *supernatural* explanation. This is naturalism, and this is how naturalists view the Bible. With these things in mind, we will look at how most naturalists and atheists view the Old Testament.

Source & Form Criticism: Alternative Theories of the Bible's Authorship

The naturalist perspective on the Old Testament is the typical scholarly worldview used to teach students about this text. In the eyes of most professors at public universities, the Old Testament is *just another ancient book of legends* based on *exaggerations* about the ancient Israelite and Jewish people and their religion. **Traditional Jews and Christians believe that <u>Moses</u> wrote the first 5 books of the Bible based on** *supernatural revelation* **that he received from God**. But this view is *firmly rejected* by *most* modern scholars—*even most Jewish and Christian scholars*. So, according to modern scholars, *who wrote the Bible?* Modern scholars with a naturalist worldview will answer this question using the academic discipline known as **<u>textual criticism</u>**.

Textual criticism is basically the practice of **challenging the traditional authorship of ancient texts** through a process of careful analysis of the text itself. This is true for *many* ancient texts *outside* of the Bible, but it is *also* applies to the Bible. For example, the ancient Greek religion of polytheism is clearly seen in the ancient text known as *The Iliad*. **Traditionally, everyone agreed that a Greek poet named Homer wrote** *The Iliad*. But textual critics *challenge this idea* and propose *alternative* authors.

When studying the Bible, scholars in more recent history have used **2 types of textual criticism: <u>source criticism</u>** and **<u>form criticism</u>**. Source criticism is a detailed analysis of the specific sources that led to the Bible's authorship. What is the **source**—or rather, *what are the sources*—of the Bible? Scholars with the naturalist worldview use the discipline of source criticism to answer this question. Going deeper, these scholars use form criticism to determine *when* specific texts in the Bible were written.

Form criticism analyzes the style that each author used to compose every individual passage of the Bible. Form criticism carefully analyzes the original language of each verse in the Old Testament to determine when these texts were written. Form criticism is what has led most scholars today to propose that Judges chapter 5 and Exodus chapter 15 are the oldest texts in the Bible. I will discuss a recent theory about this a bit more in the next volume. For now, recognize that **naturalist scholars use the practices of source and form criticism to determine who** *really* **wrote the Bible**. Naturalist scholars have *no unified theory* about who wrote the Bible. However, **they all** *agree* **that the first 5 books of the Bible** *could not have been written by Moses*.

Today, there are *many* <u>different theories</u> about *who* **wrote each part of the Bible**. Each of these theories is based on *how* different scholars apply textual criticism to the ancient literature. In this chapter, I will introduce you to **3 of the main theories used by modern scholars to determine who wrote the first 5 books of the Bible**. These first 5 books are **Genesis, Exodus, Leviticus, Numbers,** and **Deuteronomy**. Collectively, they are known as the *Torah* and the *Pentateuch*. *These books are the foundation of the Hebrew Bible's narrative.* How each person interprets these books will determine *everything else* about how they interpret the rest of the Bible.

The **first of the 3 theories** I will be discussing in this chapter is **one of the oldest** *and* **most popular theories of textual criticism relating to the Hebrew Bible**. This is known as the <u>**Documentary Hypothesis**</u>. This theory developed over the course of *many* years and took its traditional form in the late 18th century just after the Enlightenment period. This theory first began to take shape when *many* **different scholars began to use** <u>textual criticism</u> **to challenge the traditional Judeo-Christian view that Moses wrote the Torah**. These scholars began to do this by reading the Bible more carefully, using detailed analysis to determine whether or not Moses could have *actually* authored these texts.

Sadly, it is true that many people with a religious worldview *do not* read their sacred texts. Despite our unprecedented access to the

Bible, **biblical illiteracy is rampant among Christians of all backgrounds in today's world**. Scholars who study and work in the fields of history and religion read sacred texts with *high precision and detail*. In doing so, they notice *many* contradictions, inconsistencies, duplicate stories, and problematic passages within the Pentateuch. **Each of these difficult texts suggests that the Pentateuch was written by multiple authors, *not* only one author**. If this is the case, it means that Moses *did not* write the Torah.

A full account of *all* the problematic texts that naturalist scholars point to in the Bible is beyond the scope of this series. However, I will give a couple examples of these problematic texts. Some broad examples of texts that scholars consider problematic are texts that include stories that seem to copy each other, indicating that each story was originally written down by a different author. Scholars call these "*doublets*." The first doublet appears in the first 2 chapters of Genesis. A careful reading of these texts suggests that there are **2 creation stories, *not one*** (see Genesis 1:1-2:3 and Genesis 2:4-25).

A few more **examples of doublets** can be found in the story of the **Flood** (with apparent mixing of events from seemingly different authors in Genesis chapters 6-9), **God's Covenant with Abraham** (Genesis chapter 15 and Genesis chapter 17), **Abraham's lie about Sarah** (Genesis 12:10-20 and Genesis 20:1-18), and **God changing Jacob's name to Israel** (Genesis 32:25-33 and Genesis 35:9-10). Beside all the doublets in the text, there are also certain stories that contain **contradictions that make the story difficult to understand**. These contradictions suggest that the text of the Pentateuch derived from *more than one author* and editors who *worked to combine separate sources*. One of the best examples of this comes from **the story of Joseph found in Genesis chapter 37**. Pay close attention to this text, especially to the **bold**, *italicized,* and underlined portions of the story:

"And Israel said to Joseph, 'Are not your brothers pasturing the flock at Shechem? Come, I will send you to them.' And he said to him, 'Here I am.' So he said to him, 'Go now, see if it is well with your brothers and with the flock, and bring me word.' So he sent him from the Valley of Hebron, and he came to Shechem. And a man found him wandering in the fields. And the man asked him, 'What are you seeking?' 'I am seeking my brothers,' he said. 'Tell me, please, where they are pasturing the flock.' And the man said, 'They have gone away, for I heard them say, 'Let us go to Dothan.''' **So Joseph went after his brothers and found them at Dothan. They saw him from afar,** and *before he came near to them* **they conspired against him to <u>kill</u> him.** They said to one another, 'Here comes this dreamer. Come now, **let us <u>kill him</u>** *and* **throw him into one of the pits**. Then *we will say that a fierce animal has devoured him,* and we will see what will become of his dreams.' But when **Reuben** heard it, **he rescued him out of their hands**, saying, 'Let us not take his life.' And **Reuben said to them,** 'Shed no blood; *throw him into this pit here in the wilderness*, but do not lay a hand on him' — that he might rescue him out of their hand to restore him to his father. So when Joseph came to his brothers, they stripped him of his robe, the robe of many colors that he wore. And **they took him and threw him into a pit**. The pit was empty; there was no water in it. Then **they sat down to eat**. And looking up **they** saw a caravan of **<u>Ishmaelites</u>** coming from Gilead, with their camels bearing gum, balm, and myrrh, on their way to carry it down to Egypt. Then **<u>Judah</u>** said to his brothers, 'What profit is it if we kill our brother and conceal his blood?

Come, **let us sell him to the Ishmaelites**, and let not our hand be upon him, for he is our brother, our own flesh.' And his brothers listened to him. Then **Midianite traders** passed by. And *they* **drew Joseph up and lifted him out of the pit**, *and sold him to the Ishmaelites* for twenty shekels of silver. *They took Joseph to Egypt.* When **Reuben returned to the pit and saw that Joseph was not in the pit**, he tore his clothes and returned to his brothers and said, 'The boy is gone, and I, where shall I go?' Then *they took Joseph's robe and slaughtered a goat and dipped the robe in the blood.* And they sent the robe of many colors and *brought it to their father* and said, 'This we have found; please identify whether it is your son's robe or not.' And he identified it and said, 'It is my son's robe. *A fierce animal has devoured him.* Joseph is without doubt torn to pieces.' Then Jacob tore his garments and put sackcloth on his loins and mourned for his son many days. All his sons and all his daughters rose up to comfort him, but he refused to be comforted and said, 'No, I shall go down to Sheol to my son, mourning.' Thus his father wept for him. Meanwhile **the Midianites had sold him in Egypt** to **Potiphar**, an officer of Pharaoh, the captain of the guard."
Genesis 37:13-36

This story about how Joseph ended up in Egypt because of his brothers' jealousy is very popular in Sunday School. It *seems* to be straightforward — *until you read the text more slowly.* As soon as Joseph is about to make contact with his brothers, the exact text found in the Hebrew Bible begins to get confusing. The general idea of what happens to Joseph is clear, but the exact details of *how* this happened is unclear due to **multiple characters and ideas getting mixed**

together.

First, Joseph's brother's plan to kill him, but they decide not to do so. But why do Joseph's brother's change their mind? According to this story, at first it seems like **Reuben** was the one who convinced his brother not to kill Joseph. But then, only a couple verses later, *Reuben is somehow gone*, Joseph is trapped in the pit, and **Judah** has to convince Joseph's brothers not to kill him *all over again*. Who convinced Joseph's other brothers not to kill him: Reuben? Or Judah? This is the first contradiction in the text that seems to point to multiple authors of this text. But it doesn't stop there.

Next, we see the general idea and theme of Joseph being sold as a slave to Egypt. But again, exactly *how* does this happen? First, it seems like **Judah comes up with the idea to sell Joseph to Ishmaelite traders** who are passing by on their way down to Egypt. Then, out of the blue, **Midianite traders** *suddenly take Joseph out of the pit and sell him to the Ishmaelite traders* **instead of Judah and Joseph's brothers**. This is when **Reuben** *mysteriously appears back in the story*, without *any* explanation as to *why* he left Judah and his other brothers earlier in the story after he convinced them not to kill Joseph. Finally, at the end of this chapter, we read that it was **the Midianite traders**—*not the Ishmaelite traders*—**who brought Joseph down to Egypt and sold him to Potiphar**, the captain of Pharaoh's guard.

All these mixed details from the text of Genesis chapter 37 *strongly* suggest that this story was **written down and edited by** *multiple* **authors,** *not one, single author*. If this is the case, *then Moses did not write* Genesis chapter 37—at least not in the way that it appears in our Bibles today. This is *one of many texts* from the Pentateuch that scholars in the field of **textual criticism** began to use to build a case that *Moses* **did not** *write the Torah*. At first, these scholars did not have *any* unified idea about *who* wrote the Torah.

They merely proposed that *Moses was not the author*, and that **this text was written down by** *more than one* **author**.

Scholars began to apply these methods of textual criticism to come up with alternative theories of authorship for the Bible during the 1600s leading up into the Enlightenment Period. Since the 17th Century, the traditional view that Moses wrote the Pentateuch has become less and less popular in professional academic communities. In 1780, a German scholar named **Johann Eichhorn** built off the earlier work of a French scholar named **Jean Astruc** to propose the idea of **2 separate authors of the Pentateuch**. Eichhorn called these authors the "**Yahwist**" and the "**Elohimist**" — abbreviated as sources "**J**" and "**E**." Shortly after this, another German scholar named **Wilhelm de Wette** proposed a third author for the Pentateuch called the "**Deuteronomist**." He abbreviated the label of this source as "**D**." Later, "**D**" **was split into 2 separate sources**, creating the proposal of a fourth author called "**Priestly Writer**," abbreviated as "**P**."

These **4 proposed authors**, or sources, abbreviated as **J, E, D, and P**, formed the **foundation for all mainstream alternative theories for the Pentateuch's authorship from the 1800s up to the present time**. However, since that time, there has been a **significant disagreement among naturalist scholars** about *who* these authors were, *when* they wrote down their texts, and *which editors complied their works together* to form the Pentateuch as it is today. There is *some* consensus among naturalist scholars about theories relating to the sources called "**D**" and "**P**." But *most scholars in recent history and today have vastly different views about the traditional sources* identified as "**J**" and "**E**."

To answer the question of *who* wrote the Pentateuch, the **first and originally** **most popular view** among naturalist scholars was developed in the mid-1800s and afterward. It is called the

Documentary Hypothesis. It was 2 German scholars—**Hermann Hupfeld** in 1853 and **Julius Wellhausen** in 1878—who published books that solidified the dominant **popularity of the Documentary Hypothesis based on the 4 proposed authors abbreviated as JEDP**. According to this theory, *the first 5 books of the Bible were **not** written by Moses*. Instead, these books were **written by at least 4 authors with differing interests and perspectives**. The identities of these 4 authors can be abbreviated with the letters **J-E-D-P**. According to the original version of the Documentary Hypothesis Theory, these authors began writing the Old Testament during the time of King Solomon or shortly afterward. They completed their work around the time of the Babylonian Exile. **This theory proposes that most of the Old Testament was written between 970 and 586 BCE**.

Today, the Documentary Hypothesis is much less popular. It is still proposed by some scholars, but it has been largely rejected due to **new discoveries in the field of ancient Near Eastern archaeology**. One of the most prominent scholars today who embraces an updated version of the Documentary Hypothesis Theory is **Dr. Joel S. Baden**. Dr. Baden is the Professor of Hebrew Bible at Yale Divinity School. He is also one of the *few* naturalist scholars left today who believes that the stories about King David and Solomon have more connections to actual history than legend. Dr. Baden wrote a book describing his view of the Documentary Hypothesis in detail back in 2012. It is called *The Composition of the Pentateuch: Renewing the Documentary Hypothesis*. Dr. Baden's view is challenged by many other scholars today who hold to newer theories about the background behind the "J," "E," "D," and "P" sources behind the Pentateuch. Most of these other scholars propose a theory called the **Supplementary Hypothesis**.

The Supplementary Hypothesis grew up alongside the

Documentary Hypothesis for *many* years in recent history. However, **this theory surpassed the Documentary Hypothesis in popularity when it was masterfully argued by 3 different 1970s scholars: John Van Seters, Rolf Rendtorff,** and **Hans Heinrich Schmid**. In their academic works, these scholars propose *only 3 main sources for the authorship of the Pentateuch*. They argue that the Pentateuch's 3 major sources are "**D**," "**J**," and "**P**." Contrary to the view of the Documentary Hypothesis, the Supplementary Hypothesis *rejects* "*E*" *as a separate source* and **combines the suggested material for** "**E**" **with the** "**J**" **source**. For this reason, some who hold this view call this source "**JE**" instead of "**J**." Additionally, the Supplementary Hypothesis **changes the chronological order** for *when* each source first came into existence.

In the **Documentary Hypothesis**, "J" was written down *first* and *separately* from *all* the other sources. After this, "E" was written down *separately*. Later, "D" was written down *separately*. Finally, "P" wrote their work *separately*, and "**P**" **combined the separate works of** "**J**," "**E**," and "**D**" **together with their work**. Later, other editors—called *redactors*—came along and made further edits to the text until it eventually reached its final form in the Hebrew Bible we have today. **The Supplementary Hypothesis rejects this chronology and process**.

According to the Supplementary Hypothesis, "**D**" **wrote their work** *first*. Then, after "D," *another* source called "J" or "JE" edited the original writing in "D" and **added supplemental material to the text**. This supplemental material included *more ancient* songs, poems, and traditions that *may have preceded* the original writing done by "D." Finally, another editor named "P" came to add some final material to the work of "**DJ**" and finalized the Pentateuch as a work of "**D-J-P**." **Today, the Supplementary Hypothesis**—*in one form or* *another*—is the dominant view used to determine the original authorship of the Pentateuch.

An evolution of this view is held by a prominent scholar named **Dr. David M. Carr**. He refers to his perspective as the *Sources and Supplements Hypothesis*. Dr. Carr is the Professor of Hebrew Bible at Union Theological Seminary. In 2011, Dr. Carr wrote a book detailing his theory on who wrote the Pentateuch. This book is called *The Formation of the Hebrew Bible: A New Reconstruction*.

There is a third, *newer* theory that has been proposed in recent years that modifies and goes beyond *both* the Documentary *and* Supplementary Hypotheses. *There is no mainstream name for this new theory yet.* However, some, such as Dr. Matt Baker, refer to this as the **Dual Origins Hypothesis**. This theory is *heavily* based on a book written in 2010 by Dr. Konrad Schmid called *Genesis and the Moses Story: Israel's Dual Origins in the Hebrew Bible*. Dr. Konrad Schmid is the Professor of Hebrew Bible and Ancient Judaism at the University of Zurich. **The Dual Origins Hypothesis uses a mix of textual criticism and newer information in the field of ancient Near Eastern archaeology to propose 2 separate mainstream sources that eventually combined to form the Pentateuch and the Hebrew Bible as a whole**.

In the narrative of the Hebrew Bible, there is a United Kingdom of Israel that *eventually* **splits into 2 separate kingdoms** called <u>Israel</u> and <u>Judah</u>. Archaeology has clearly identified the historical reality of *both* the Northern Kingdom of Israel and the Southern Kingdom of Judah. However, there is *very* little—*if any*—archaeological evidence that can support the Hebrew Bible's story of a grand, powerful United Kingdom of Israel. Based on this, many scholars have begun proposing that *there never was a United Kingdom of Israel*.

According to the Dual Origins Hypothesis, **the Northern**

Kingdom of Israel and the Southern Kingdom of Judah originated *separately* from each other. The Northern Kingdom of Israel was greater *and* more powerful in history than the Southern Kingdom of Judah. However, the Northern Kingdom of Israel *rapidly* declined and collapsed under the Assyrian Empire. **Refugees from the Northern Kingdom of Israel were absorbed into the Southern Kingdom of Judah.** During the reign of King Hezekiah, this Southern Kingdom of Judah grew *exponentially* when Israel fell in the North. **Both the Hebrew Bible *and* archaeology vividly confirm these events.** As a result, naturalist scholars argue that the historical, archaeological reality points to a **United Kingdom of Judah that *incorporated* more ancient traditions from the lost Kingdom of Northern Israel.**

With this view in mind, the **Dual Origins Hypothesis** describes **the Pentateuch as a compilation of written sources that originated from *both* the Northern Kingdom of Israel *and* the Southern Kingdom of Judah.** In this theory, the traditional "JE" source or "J" source was written down *first* in **2** *different versions*. The **Northern Israelite version** focused on the origin story of **Israel**, **Moses**, and the **exodus from Egypt**. However, the **Southern Kingdom of Judah's version** focused on the origin story of **3 patriarchs: Abraham, Isaac,** and **Jacob**. The original text composed in Judah emphasized *Aaron* as a hero, the *Zadokite* priesthood, *Judah* as the most important *forefather*, *Jacob* as Judah's father, and cultural connections to *Mesopotamia*. The original text composed in Northern Israel emphasized *Moses* as a hero, the *Levite* priesthood, *Joseph* as the most important *forefather*, *Israel* as Joseph's father, and cultural connections to *Egypt*.

In the Dual Origins Hypothesis, **Jacob and Israel were originally viewed as *separate* ancestors.** Jacob was the ancestor of the people of Judah, and Israel was the ancestor of the people of Israel. **When these 2 separate kingdoms combined in Judah after the fall of Northern Israel, the originally separate traditions of Jacob and Israel merged together** *also*. In the Dual Origins Hypothesis, the "D" source was originally written *separately* near the fall of the Northern Kingdom of Israel. Then, when the Israelite refugees became citizens of the Southern Kingdom of Judah, professional scribes (or one scribe) used *all* the textual sources of "JE" from *both* the Northern and Southern Kingdoms **to create a unified text. This project was completed by the "P" source.** Eventually, at a later time, **another redactor combined the full work of "P" with the older work of "D."** According to the Dual Origins Hypothesis, this final compilation is the basis for the Pentateuch we have today.

The main point to take away from all this information is that **naturalist scholars *reject* traditional views about the Bible.** They *do not* believe Moses wrote *any* part of the Bible, and many of them *do not even believe there was a historical Moses.* **Most naturalist scholars base their views on the philosophies of modernism and humanism.** Furthermore, many naturalist scholars come from religious backgrounds and embrace various forms of Judaism and Christianity. **It is important for you to know that the naturalist worldview, colored by modernism and humanism, is the dominant worldview held by most people today** — *even people of faith*. This is why it is important to know how naturalist scholars view the Bible and its origins. Here is a ***list of prominent naturalist scholars today*** who have made major contributions to the study of the Hebrew Bible. For more information about their views, you can turn to these individuals for further research:

1. Dr. **Joel S. Baden**, *Professor of Hebrew Bible at Yale Divinity School.*

2. Dr. **David M. Carr**, *Professor of Hebrew Bible at Union Theological Seminary.*

3. Dr. **Konrad Schmid**, *Professor of Hebrew Bible and Ancient Judaism at the University of Zurich.*

4. Dr. **William M. Schniedewind**, *Professor of Biblical Studies and Northwest Semitic Languages at University of California in Los Angeles (UCLA).*

5. Dr. **Israel Finkelstein**, *Israeli Archaeologist, Professor Emeritus at Tel Aviv University, and the Head of the School of Archaeology and Maritime Cultures at the University of Haifa.*

6. Dr. **Christine Hayes**, *Sterling Professor of Religious Studies in Classical Judaica at Yale University.*

7. Dr. **Francesca Stavrakopoulou**, *Professor of Hebrew Bible and Ancient Religion in the Department of Theology and Religion at University of Exeter.*

8. Dr. **Daniel E. Fleming**, *Ethel and Irvin A. Edelman Professor of Hebrew and Judaic Studies and Senior Fellow of the Institute for the Study of the Ancient World at New York University.*

9. Dr. **Brendon C. Benz**, *Associate Professor of History and Theologian-in-Residence at William Jewell College.*

10. Dr. **Joshua Bowen** and **Megan Lewis**, *Professional Scholars and Hosts of the Digital Hammurabi Podcast.*

11. Dr. **Matt Baker**, *Founder and Owner of UsefulCharts, a company that designs and sells infographic posters to promote education, and the Main Host of the UsefulCharts YouTube Channel.*

In this section, I have presented **3 *main views* that most naturalist scholars today use to answer the question of the Pentateuch's original authorship**:

1. **The Documentary Hypothesis**
2. **The Supplementary Hypothesis**
3. **The Dual Origins Hypothesis**

As I mentioned previously, the Documentary Hypothesis is *no longer the dominant view of naturalist scholars*. This is primarily *due to more recent discovers in ancient Near Eastern archaeology* that were unearthed between the 1900s and the present time. Nevertheless, the Documentary Hypothesis was the original, primary explanation that naturalist scholars in recent history used to determine *who* wrote the Pentateuch. It forms the foundation for the building that is modern source and form criticism. For this reason, it is important to understand the Documentary Hypothesis in more detail. Before we move on to discuss other subjects that influence how naturalist scholars view the Bible, I will spend a little more time describing the details of the classic Documentary Hypothesis.

Authors J, E, D, and P in the Documentary Hypothesis

In the original version of the **Documentary Hypothesis**, the **4 authors of the Pentateuch** included the **Yahwist (J)**, the **Elohimist (E)**, the **Deuteronomist (D)**, and the **Priestly Writer (P)**. Each of these 4 authors **wrote at different periods of ancient Hebrew history between 970 and the 500s BCE**. The *Yahwist was the earliest author.* He is recognized for the way he frequently uses the divine name *"Yahweh"* or *"Jehovah"* to record his history of events. This is the sacred name of the Jewish God. This name is translated into English Bibles using the title: *"The LORD"* in all capital letters. The *Elohimist is the second author*, and he is recognized by his preference of the *other* divine name: *"El"* or *"Elohim."* This is translated into English as *"God."* These first 2 authors emphasize the different names of God.

The third and fourth authors emphasize more *practical* concerns of the ancient Hebrew religion. **The Deuteronomist author focused on the subject of covenant and the laws, or commandments, that were associated with the covenant**. For example, this author emphasizes the command not to have any other gods beside the One God of Israel. Finally, **the Priestly author focuses on the ritual traditions of purity connected with the ancient Hebrew community**. These traditions are frequently seen in the *Book of Leviticus*.

In addition to these first 4 authors, *<u>other authors and editors came together to complete the original text that became the Old Testament</u>*. In this theory, the first 5 books of the Bible were **written by a team of many authors**. Each of these authors **lived in different points of ancient history**. With that in mind, this view rejects that the first 5 books of the Bible were written by Moses. *Some who hold* this view question whether or not there <u>ever was</u> a man named Moses. Future naturalist scholars, such as those who are prominent today, would use these 4 authors (**J**, **E**, **D**, and **P**) to refer to the major sources of the Pentateuch in new theories.

The Yahwist (J)

According to the original Documentary Hypothesis, the *earliest author* of the Old Testament was the **Yahwist**. He **wrote sometime around 850 BCE** or shortly beforehand—with older scholars suggesting that he *could have written as early as the 900s BCE*. Older scholars suggested that **he began writing at the height of the United Kingdom of Israel during the reign of King Solomon**. But as historical criticism of the Bible's narrative increased, scholars began to think **he wrote *after* the kingdom was divided in the North and South**. I will discuss more about the historical background and narrative of the Old Testament later. But for now, I will make brief references to it for the purpose of explaining this theory.

According to the original Documentary Hypothesis, this author **began writing his content at Genesis 2:4**. This is seen as **the *original* narrative of the creation of the world and humanity**. This came *before* **a later author added the first chapter of Genesis and the first verses of chapter 2**. This "**J**" author wrote most of the *Book of Genesis* and some parts of the *Books of Exodus* and *Numbers*. This author had a *very* personal view of God. He was **less interested in the later Hebrew laws and customs** shown in *Leviticus* and *Deuteronomy*. One passage from the Bible used to support the theory of this author is **Genesis 4:26**. This verse says:

"To Seth also a son was born, and he called his name Enosh. At that time people began to call upon **the name of the LORD.**"

Here you can see the divine name "*Yahweh*" which is translated as "**the LORD**" in English. The "J" author emphasized this divine name for the God of Israel. **In the Supplementary Hypothesis, this source is combined with the "E" author.** Also in the Supplementary Hypothesis, this "JE" author was an *editor* or *redactor* **of the original "D" author's larger writing. He took a collection of more ancient songs, poems, and oral traditions and wove them into the "D" author's work around 540 BCE, near the end of the Babylonian Exile.**

In the Documentary Hypothesis, this "J" author is one of the 4 authors who composed completed, separate documents that were originally edited and compiled into one document that became the Pentateuch. In the Supplementary Hypothesis, this "J" or "JE" author **did not create** *any* **original document**. Instead, he merely **supplemented the original document** that was created by the "D" author at an earlier time in history. In the Dual Origins Hypothesis, the "JE" source has **2 separate origins**: one in the **Northern Kingdom of Israel** and one in the **Southern Kingdom of Judah**. After the fall of the Northern Kingdom of Israel, a scribe *or* group of scribes combined the 2 separate traditions from the "JE" sources in Israel and Judah to create a main body of literature that would evolve into the Pentateuch.

The Elohimist (E)

According to the original Documentary Hypothesis, the *second earliest author* of the Old Testament was the **Elohimist**. This author is *the most contested* in more recent scholarship. Among those who argue for the Documentary Hypothesis, some would say that this second author **wrote his own original document** that was eventually found by an editor and combined with the earlier "J" author's document. But others would argue that this "E" author was an editor who somehow found the writings of the "J" author and decided to add to his work. In this other view, this author was **the first redactor**. This means that he was the first author who took the original written work from the Yahwist author, edited it, added more content, and then published a second version of the text. This author is viewed as the one who **produced the second edition of the Hebrew Bible**.

In the classic Documentary Hypothesis view, this "E" author began his work around Genesis chapter 15. **Those who propose this theory and promote it admit that it is often** *difficult to distinguish between the writings of the Yahwist* **(J)** *and Elohimist* (E). But in the minds of older scholars and perhaps some scholars today who still accept the Documentary Hypothesis, this "E" author viewed God as a *more* **distant** and **sovereign** figure. This "E" author viewed God as more concerned about morality than personal relationships. This is in stark contrast to the "J" author's view of God. To this "E" author, God is a perfect yet fierce being called *Elohim*. To the former "J" author, God is a relatable, pro-human deity called *Yahweh*. The Bible verse used to support this theory comes from **Exodus 3:15**. In this verse, the English translation "**God**" covers over the Hebrew name "*Elohim.*" **In Hebrew,** *Elohim* **is another major name of God throughout the Old Testament.**

In the original view of the Documentary Hypothesis, the "E" author **wrote his part of the Hebrew Bible around 750 BCE in the Northern territory of the divided kingdom.** *This was the Northern*

Kingdom called Israel. As I mentioned previously, more recent scholarship mainly rejects the "E" author altogether. Going in line with the Supplementary Hypothesis, they would propose that this "E" author is **the same as the "J" author, and their work was written around 540 BCE during the Babylonian Exile as a supplement to the earlier work that had previously been completed by the "D" author**. However, the **Dual Origins Hypothesis allows for 2 separate documents** — or *at least 2 separate oral traditions with smaller written collections* — to originate in the Northern Kingdom of Israel that would eventually be combined with the document or collections in the Southern Kingdom of Judah. Nevertheless, this would be *the only distinction between the 2 sources*. The Dual Origins Hypothesis would *not* label these 2 sources as "J" and "E," as is the case with the Documentary Hypothesis.

The Deuteronomist (D)

According to the original Documentary Hypothesis, the *third original author* of the Old Testament is known as the **Deuteronomist**. As with the "E" author, this "D" author either wrote his own original document that was later combined with the other 3 sources to form the Pentateuch, or he wrote additions to a single existing document. Whatever the case may be, this "D" author **wrote his text around 621 BCE during the reign of King Josiah in the Southern Kingdom of Judah**. This was the author of most of the *Book of Deuteronomy*. If this author was editing and adding content to another original document that came from the authors "J" and "E," then he was the **second redactor of the text**. He composed **the third edition of the Old Testament**.

The content of this "D" author's writing suggests that his focus was firmly fixed on **morality** and the conditional yet **special covenant which God had with the people of Israel**. This "D" author's content is the main foundation for the **theme of the Hebrew Bible** that carries on *after* the Pentateuch. His work is the beginning of what naturalist scholars call the *"Deuteronomistic History."* This refers to the Hebrew Bible's narrative of how the Israelites could *never* protect Yahweh's Covenant and continually rejected Him by worshipping other gods.

In the Supplementary Hypothesis, this "D" author wrote the one and *only* main document that was edited *many* times and supplemented before becoming the Pentateuch. In the view of the Supplementary Hypothesis, this "D" author **wrote his main document within the 600s BCE**, perhaps **around 600 BCE**. In the Supplementary Hypothesis, this "D" author is the primary, main author of the Pentateuch. However, his work would later be **supplemented by the works of "JE" around 540 BCE and then by "P" around 400 BCE** when it would become the Pentateuch. In the Dual Origins Hypothesis, this "D" author composed his text *separately* from the "JE" author in the Northern Kingdom of Israel. After the 2 separate sources and traditions of "JE" were combined in the Southern Kingdom of Judah by the Priestly Writer (P), another redactor came along and added this "D" source to create the Pentateuch.

The Priestly Writer (P) and Other Editors (R)

According to the original Documentary Hypothesis, the *fourth and final original author* of the Old Testament was the **Priestly Writer**. He **wrote sometime around 500 BCE shortly** *after* **the time of the Babylonian Exile**. By that time, the Jews lived in foreign lands after they had been deported from their homeland in the previous century. **This "P" author was *either the first or third redactor* of the Old Testament text.** According to the original Documentary Hypothesis, this "P" author composed original work that he added to the Pentateuch. However, he was *also* the one who **finalized the first 5 books of the Bible**. He published them as they appear today.

In the view of the original Documentary Hypothesis, this "P" author made his own additions to the text of the Old Testament. He **wrote the first chapter of Genesis and the first few verses of the second chapter to create the second creation narrative**. He *also* wrote the entire *Book of Leviticus*. Like the "E" author, this author *also* preferred the divine name of *Elohim* for God. **Exodus 6:3** is a supporting text for this theory. It says:

> "*I appeared to Abraham, to Isaac, and to Jacob, as God Almighty* [Hebrew: ***El Shaddai***], *but by my name the LORD* [Hebrew: **YaHWeH**] *I did not make myself known to them.*"

According to the original Documentary Hypothesis, these 4 main authors of the Pentateuch had *other unknown authors* help them in their completion of the text. As this text was passed from generation to generation among the ancient Hebrews, these **other authors added to it and refined it to make it what it is today**. These other authors each shared views that reflected those of the 4 main authors. Those who propose this theory see Genesis chapter 14 as an example of a text that was written by one of the unknown authors. In the Documentary Hypothesis view, these unknown authors are called **Redactors**, abbreviated with an "**R**." The **redactors added fragments to the evolving piece of literature that became the Pentateuch over time between the eras of the "J" and "P" authors**. In the end, it was the "P" author who was responsible for the *fourth and final edition of the original Hebrew Bible*.

One primary criticism of the Documentary Hypothesis throughout recent history has been its need for *many* redactors, or "R" editors, to explain the Pentateuch in its final form. How could the very diverse worldviews of the "J," "E," "D," and "P" sources be combined by *so many* different redactors in history? The Supplementary Hypothesis answers this by getting rid of the "E" author altogether and proposing *only 3 major authors of the text*. In the Supplementary Hypothesis, the "D" source is the original author, while the "JE" and "P" sources use supplemental material from *many* unknown authors to complete the text. It is also the "P" and the "R" editors who publish *the final version of the Pentateuch* in the Supplementary Hypothesis *and* the Dual Origins Hypothesis. Ultimately, **each of these 3 main naturalist theories of the Pentateuch's authorship show that while the Pentateuch had** *more than one author*, **the** *exact* **number of authors and editors is unknown**.

Whichever naturalist theory of authorship scholars may choose, the main point is one of negation: *Moses did* <u>*not*</u> *write the Pentateuch*. The number of alternative theories of the Pentateuch's history and authorship seems endless. As the discipline of studying the Bible from a naturalist worldview became more popular in recent history, scholars began turning to archaeology to answer questions about the Bible's troublesome passages. **Textual criticism began to be enhanced by the discipline of historical criticism, and historical criticism was revolutionized by new discoveries in ancient Near Eastern archaeology.**

Remember, **naturalist scholars are humanists and modernists**. They believe that absolute truth can be *fully* known and understood through a process of careful scholarly research and discussion leading to a point of unified consensus. In this worldview, the Bible's story is *not* a good source to learn about *real* history. In their view, the Bible is an ***ancient text*** that is not much different than *The Iliad* that derived from ancient Greek culture. No one in the modern world would use *The Iliad* as a **primary** source to learn about history. Instead, modern scholars prefer to find real, material objects in the ground through archaeology. Then, they use scientific data and technology to test the legitimacy of these findings. In doing these things, **naturalist scholars challenge traditional views of history**. This is called <u>**historical criticism**</u>.

Rejecting Moses' authorship of the Pentateuch, the Bible's *foundational* narrative, is only the beginning of how naturalist scholars view the Bible and its background. Naturalist scholars take their perspective even further by combining their insights from both textual and historical criticism. They use troublesome passages in the Hebrew Bible's text and archaeological discoveries to reconstruct what they would argue is a more accurate picture of ancient Near Eastern history. In their view, the Israelites of the Bible were born out of the ancient culture and religion of the Canaanites.

Older naturalist scholars originally *doubted* that the Canaanite religion mentioned in the Bible ever *existed*, but this changed with the archaeological discoveries at the ancient port city of <u>**Ugarit**</u> and elsewhere. After these discoveries, **scholars saw that the religion of the ancient Hebrews was somehow connected to the Ugaritic religion. The Ugaritic religion refers to the ancient paganism practiced by the Canaanites mentioned in the Bible.** According to modern scholars at most public schools today, **Judaism evolved over the course of hundreds of years from the ancient religion of Ugarit.** In the mind of naturalist scholars, the Old Testament is an important source for insight into this ancient pagan religion.

The Origin of Ancient Israel & Their Pagan Practices

Naturalist scholars base their views on archaeology and textual criticism. However, archeological discoveries and historical texts outside the Bible have shed much light on the Hebrew Bible's content. Sometimes these extrabiblical sources bring to light uncomfortable realities. Both secular and religious scholars today point out that the **ancient Israelites adopted the religious traditions of the ancient Canaanites who lived around them.** *The Bible itself exposes this fact,* and it is **true** *even when the Bible is interpreted literally in every area.* But when did the Israelites adopt Canaanite religion, and how deep does this connection go? The answer to this question is the difference between modern scholars who are naturalist and those who are not. Here I will present the views of naturalist Bible scholars that challenge the content in the Hebrew Bible.

Much of the historical background of the stories in the Old Testament is shrouded in mystery. How this mystery is **interpreted** depends on one's worldview. **Naturalist scholars view history from the perspective of evolution.** In addition to holding a worldview revolving around evolution, naturalist scholars use the academic field of **archaeology** to construct their idea of ancient human history. In this worldview, humanity evolved from lower lifeforms over the course of millions of years. Once humanity became separate from other species, the Stone Age began.

In the **Stone Age**, humans were all **primitive** creatures. They lived in caves and used **stone tools**. They didn't have any farming systems, but they used processes of **hunting and gathering** to survive. Near the end of the Stone Age, humanity developed **agriculture**: the process of farming. This slowly began the development the most ancient human civilizations. Then, humanity learned how to create **metal**. The first metal they created was **bronze**. At this point, they began using **bronze tools instead of stone tools**. This began the period known as the **Bronze Age**.

The Bronze Age lasted from around **3300 BCE to 1200 BCE**. The Bronze Age was a period of advanced human societies. Archaeological evidence reveals **multiple advanced civilizations** that thrived in the Bronze Age. Some of these include the earliest Sumerians, Egyptians, Babylonians, Amorites, Assyrians, Greeks, Indus River Valley peoples, and even the Chinese. Many of these civilizations, especially those situated on the east coast of the Mediterranean Sea and further into the Middle East, had contact with each other. They developed sophisticated systems of **trade**, systems of **writing**, and central **governments**.

Naturalist scholars generally do not favor the Bible's testimony about the origin of the people of Israel. Instead, they favor archaeological evidence and historical interpretations based in the evolutionary worldview. For this reason, naturalist scholars want to know what we can learn about Israel outside the Bible. Outside the Bible, a people called "**Israel**" is first mentioned in an Egyptian monument called the **Merneptah Stele**. This monument was created by the Egyptian Pharaoh Merneptah as a celebration and memorial to his victory over many people who lived in the ancient Near East in the 1200s BCE. One of the people that Pharaoh Merneptah conquered is called "<u>Israel</u>."

The Merneptah Stele dates to **around 1208 BCE**. For most naturalist scholars, the Merneptah Stele **proves that the ancient Israelite people existed by the late Bronze Age**. This suggests that the origins of the people of Israel are directly connected to the history of the Bronze Age. This raises *many* problems for those who seek to know the origin of Israel outside the Bible. Around 1200 BCE — or shortly before and after this date — a *major* historical shift occurred. This event is known as the **Bronze Age Collapse**.

Many people today are familiar with the recent **dark age** that happened after the fall of the western Roman Empire. This period of history is usually called the "**Middle Ages**" or "**Medieval Times**" or the "**Dark Ages**." It began when the advanced civilization of the Roman Empire collapsed in western Europe. The reasons for the collapse are only partially understood, but it included a combination of economic problems, social decline, and foreign invasion. This period, which lasted from around 500 to 1500 CE, is called a "dark age" due to the way that human civilization seems to have gone backwards during this timeframe. Technology, knowledge, and culture declined during this timeframe. **The Bronze Age Collapse was the same type of situation, except it happened *before* the Roman Empire and *after* the ancient Egyptian Empire**.

Historians do not fully understand what caused the Bronze Age Collapse. However, as with the fall of the Roman Empire in western Europe that would happen many centuries later, the Bronze Age Collapse seems to have been caused by a combination of **economic problems**, **social decline**, and **foreign invasions**. It seems that **weather changes and environmental disasters** may have also brought about the Bronze Age Collapse. The "**Sea Peoples**," possibly connected to the group known as the **Philistines** in the Bible, also seem to have played a major role in causing the Bronze Age Collapse.

Some civilizations recovered from the Bronze Age Collapse — such as the Assyrians, Babylonians, and Persians. However, many great civilizations were put into as state of permanent decline and eventual loss due to the Bronze Age Collapse—most notable among these is the **Egyptian Empire**. The Hittite Empire is another example of a civilization that could not recover from the Bronze Age Collapse. But even more than advanced ancient civilizations, the Bronze Age Collapse led to the **loss of much ancient literature and culture**.

There are many **books referenced as sources for the Hebrew Bible** that are completely lost in history. It seems that these books were *originally* **part of the Hebrew Bible**. But somehow, these books were lost, destroyed, or purposefully abandoned. What happened to these books is ultimately a mystery. However, their loss could be connected to the Bronze Age Collapse. This chart shows **the lost books of the Hebrew Bible** that are mentioned in the Hebrew Bible:

Lost Books	References in the Bible
Book of the Covenant (Original Version)	Exodus 24:7
Book of the Wars of YHWH	Numbers 21:14
Book of Jasher	Joshua 10:13 2 Samuel 1:17-18
Book of the Manner of the Kingdom	1 Samuel 10:25
Book of the Annals of King David	1 Chronicles 27:24
Book of Samuel the Seer (Original Version)	1 Chronicles 29:29
Book of Nathan the Prophet	1 Chronicles 29:29 2 Chronicles 9:29
Book of Gad the Seer	1 Chronicles 29:29
Book of Ahijah the Shilonite	2 Chronicles 9:29

Book of Iddo the Seer	2 Chronicles 9:29
	2 Chronicles 12:15
	2 Chronicles 13:22
Book of the Acts of Solomon	1 Kings 11:41
Book of Shemaiah the Prophet	2 Chronicles 12:15
Book of Jehu	2 Chronicles 20:34
Book of the Acts of Uzziah	2 Chronicles 26:22
Book of the Sayings of the Seers	2 Chronicles 33:18-19

One of the main reasons that the origin of Israel outside the Bible is shrouded in mystery is probably the Bronze Age Collapse. However, even with the Bronze Age Collapse, the text of the Hebrew Bible and archaeology provide naturalist scholars with clues about the origin of Israel. The **people** that became known as Israel **originated in the Levant**—a region of land on the east coast of the Mediterranean Sea that stretches from modern-day Turkey in the north to modern-day Egypt in the south. They are somehow connected with the **Canaanites**, an ancient people and culture that would later evolve into the colonialist **Phoenician people**.

Archaeological findings from the ancient Levant indicate that the people who lived in this region shared a common language and culture. As with the Indigenous American peoples that were displaced by the European colonists who landed in the Americas, **the ancient Levantine peoples seem to have had diverse tribes among themselves**. But to an outsider, these different tribes may have looked *no different* from each other. *The Bible's distinction between Canaanites, Israelites, Moabites, Edomites, and all the other Levantine groups listed may have been politically contrived to separate between newer and older governments in the land.* Recent genetic analyses taken from ancient tombs *all over* the Levant from *different* time periods in ancient history reveal that **all the ancient Semitic and Levantine peoples were** *related* **to each other**. The Canaanites, Israelites, Moabites, Edomites, and all the other tribes are somehow **genetically** connected to each other.

All these things suggest that ancient Canaan and ancient Israel may have been the same group of people. However, this singular group of people must have changed their sense of identity over time as older tribes were lost and new tribes emerged among them. Based on one reading of Judges chapter 5, some textual critics among naturalist scholars point out that it seems there was **an earlier version of the people of Israel that only had 9 tribes,** *not* **12**. In their interpretation of this text and the Bible's future editions, some of these *original 9 tribes* were viewed as *outsiders*. Some naturalist scholars theorize that **the people** that the Bible calls "**Israel**" were originally a *new* **political entity** that *excluded* certain other Levantine peoples that shared a cultural and historical background in the land. The Bible's "*12 Tribes of Israel*" were the editors' politically motivated **myth** to describe the legitimate tribes of the ancient government that would eventually produce the Hebrew Bible.

One prominent naturalist scholar who writes and talks about these ideas is Dr. Daniel F. Fleming. In 2012, Fleming published a book called *The Legacy of Israel in Judah's Bible: History, Politics, and the Reinscribing of Tradition*. In this book, Fleming presents the view that **the people of Israel and Judah were originally 2** *separate* **groups**. He argues *against* the Bible's presentation that Israel and Judah came from a shared family origin. Fleming and other naturalist scholars with him use archaeological discoveries combined with textual issues in the Bible to suggest that the **Southern Kingdom of Judah**, led by the dynasty of the famous **King David, was** *originally* **small and insignificant**. Contrarily, archaeological evidence displays the glory and prominence of the Northern Kingdom of Israel — *especially during the royal dynasty of King Omri*. While the Hebrew Bible emphasizes King David's significance, archaeology and written records from the ancient Near East outside the Bible emphasize the significance of **King Omri**. The Bible reveals that Israel and Judah were somehow connected to each other through the legendary figure known as *King David*. Outside the Bible, there is *almost no archaeological evidence* that King David existed.

In the view of Fleming and many other naturalist scholars, **the separate political entities of Israel and Judah merged in history to become one people when the Northern Kingdom of Israel declined and fell into ruin during the rapid rise of the Assyrian Empire**. Before this, Judah was *insignificant* to and *separate* from the political entity that was ancient Israel. Figures like King Omri were the *original* greatest heroes, and figures like King David were originally insignificant. However, David was *somehow* connected to Judah, yet he reigned as a king of Israel *before* Israel fell apart. In the eyes of naturalist scholars, this is what helped the Kingdom of Judah invent *myths* about their heroic **King David and his *legendary* unified kingdom of Israel**. Naturalist scholars argue that such a kingdom *never existed*. They insist that archaeological evidence *does not* and *cannot* support the Bible's descriptions of the reign of King David *or* King Solomon. Instead, they suggest that the text hints at a hidden history of ancient Israel in which King David was a minor figure, while King Omri was a major one.

The Hebrew Bible's content demonstrates a strong political agenda that advances King David and his royal dynasty above all others in ancient Israelite history. As we will discuss a bit more later, the Bible describes the Temple of Israel's God, **Yahweh**, being located *only* in **Jerusalem**. Jerusalem was the royal city associated with King David and his dynasty. What the Bible *does not* describe, but what archaeology has **revealed**, is that **King Omri built a Temple of Yahweh in Samaria**. Samaria was Omri's capital city, and his royal dynasty promoted *this* location. For this reason, many naturalist scholars suggest that those who compiled the official versions of the Hebrew Bible were those who supported the political agenda linked with King David and his royal dynasty that was centered in Jerusalem. In their view, the historically *insignificant* King David won out over the more historically prominent King Omri due to the masterful literary compilation and extensive editing that created the Hebrew Bible.

King Omri, like most other ancient Israelite kings, led the people of Israel in **worshipping *many* different pagan gods**. **They *did not* worship only one God alone**. Their people and culture mostly *rejected* monotheism. These are historical facts that are supported by *both* the **Bible** *and* **archaeology**. However, this *does not* mean that the Bible's testimony is false. Remember, naturalist scholars see the Old Testament as an outdated religious text in the same way that Christians today view Homer's *Iliad*. For this reason, these scholars have come up with different theories about the true origin of Abrahamic monotheism among the ancient Hebrews. These theories are significant for us to consider since they propose a source for the worldview that evolved to become the religion of Judaism today. Naturalist and traditional Bible scholars each view the origins of the Jewish people and their faith *very* differently.

The Bible's story states that the original founder of the people of Israel was a man who came from the land of Sumer. This **patriarch** of the Israelites came to settle as a **nomad in the land of Canaan and in the land of Egypt** depending on the state of agricultural prosperity in each generation. The Israelites began as a

smaller nomadic group of people. They progressed into a thriving cultural center as they became the dominant group in the land of Canaan over the course of hundreds of years.

The traditional view of the Bible is that the people of Israel were a separate group of people from the Canaanites that lived around them. But most scholars in the naturalist worldview reject this perspective. Instead, they have found evidence which they use to argue that the Israelites arose from a large mix of nomadic tribes that lived in the territory of the ancient Phoenician peoples. This would mean that the ancient Israelites shared the language and culture of the Phoenicians in their earliest origins. The Bible characters Joseph and Moses are key exceptions to this general trend since they were both linked with Egyptian pharaohs.

Eventually, around the time of King David, the nation of Israel emerged as a separate group from the rest of the Canaanites around them. Some argue that the tribes of Israel were just specific Phoenician or Canaanite groups with religious and cultural differences. In this view, the most ancient Israelites were just *divergent Canaanites* whose presence in the Canaanite territory went back hundreds or thousands of years. A supporting historical event for this theory is the split of the Kingdom of Israel after David's son, Solomon, died. **Such division among the Israelites is thought to reveal that they were never *really* a unique people separate from the Canaanites.**

But after David became a prominent leader among the people and succeeded in uniting them, everything slowly began to change. The culture of the tribe of Judah outlived all the other tribes. The people from Judah became known as Jews, and they *strictly* adhered to their specific variations of evolved Canaanite culture. Some scholars believe this solidified the future view that the Canaanites and Israelites were always *separate* groups of people.

Modern scholars dissect the origins of Judeo-Christian faith based on this view that the Israelites in the Bible were nothing more than the dominant form of Canaanite culture. They attempt to cut down the tree of this faith by scrutinizing these pagan roots which have been exposed through archeological evidence. They argue that Abrahamic monotheism as it exists today derived from a mixture of Egyptian, Sumerian, and Canaanite religions. They say that most of the names of the God of Israel came from the Canaanite religion. Meanwhile, the concept of monotheism originated partially in ancient Sumerian religion and mainly in the ancient Egyptian religion. Ancient writings outside the Bible reveal that the Canaanite religion was influenced by the ancient religions of the Egyptian and Sumerian people. Before the ideas that developed into monotheism arose in the collective ancient consciousness, every society embraced polytheism as the dominant, mainstream religion.

The Origin of Monotheism

The dominant religion of the ancient world was polytheism. Other religions which rejected polytheism likely existed, but they were marginalized and largely rejected by mainstream society. **Polytheism is the worship of many different gods which competed for superiority**. Modern scholars theorize that polytheism originated from the earlier ancient religion of **animism**.

Animism is the view that *everything* in the world is alive, *even objects around us that appear to be motionless*. As human civilization developed and social structures changed, animism eventually became more refined and evolved into sophisticated systems of **polytheism**. This evolution of religion reflected the transformation of value systems in ancient societies. Each new system of polytheism was dependent upon the value systems of the culture in which it originated.

In the same way, **some modern scholars view monotheism as a gradually** *refined* **form of polytheism based on new social structures and value systems**. There is evidence for this type of evolution of religion in ancient texts. As polytheism evolved in certain places of the world, sometimes 2 or 3 *different* gods would merge into *one new god*. For example, in ancient Egypt, the gods called Ra and Amun were each worshipped *separately* at first. In later periods of Egyptian history, these 2 separate gods were *combined* **into one new deity**. Both Ra and Amun were considered the sun god, and the sun god came to occupy the highest status in the ancient Egyptian pantheon.

In the 1300s BCE, an Egyptian Pharaoh named **Akhenaten** mysteriously started a religious revolution in Egypt. This pharaoh got rid of all the worship of other gods *except one* **sun god** called **Amun-Ra**. The name Amun-Ra is a combination of the previously separate gods, Amun and Ra. Rather than being separate gods, this pharaoh championed the revolutionary idea that these were 2 names referring to the *same god*. Furthermore, this pharaoh gave his one god a new name: **Aten**.

This pharaoh created an Egyptian priesthood dedicated to worshipping Aten as the one true god, and *all other gods became forbidden in Egypt during his reign*. But after this pharaoh died, the next ruler of Egypt pronounced him as a **heretic** and returned Egypt to its traditional polytheism. Some speculate that the Israelites lived in Egypt around the same time that this mysterious pharaoh converted his country to strict monotheism. Since this is a likely possibility, scholars today debate how the ancient Israelites may or may not have been influenced by this seemingly **random period of ancient Egyptian monotheism**.

Traditional Jewish and Christian scholars would argue that this monotheistic Egyptian pharaoh was inspired to worship only one God because of his introduction to the One True God of Israel. This would have happened either through the events of the story of Joseph in the *Book of Genesis* or through the events of the Exodus story in the Bible. But **scholars who embrace the naturalist philosophy argue that the Israelites may have gained their idea of monotheism from Pharaoh Akhenaten**.

Some argue that Moses was influenced by the monotheistic priesthood in ancient Egypt which went underground after Pharaoh Akhenaten died. In this view, Moses' marginal faith in Egyptian monotheism was proclaimed as heresy, but Moses remained loyal to this new faith anyway and led others to follow him in it. Since Moses is seen as the enforcer of monotheism in the prophetic tradition of future Israelites, this view is supported by some people today.

The Canaanite Connection

Based on the Bible's words, the Israelites *never* worshipped the Egyptian god called Aten *or* Ra *or* Amun. Instead, **the Israelites worshipped a God Who the Bible calls both *Yahweh* and *Elohim*.** *Yahweh* is typically **translated** into **English Bibles** today as **"the LORD"** and *Elohim* is translated as **"God."** *Elohim* is the plural form of the word *"El"* in Hebrew. It is in this name *El* that scholars see a *direct connection* between the God of Israel and the ancient Canaanite religion.

The Canaanite religion centered around the ancient **Cult of El**. This was an extinct religious tradition that was discovered through the archeological findings at the ancient port city of **Ugarit**. This Ugaritic or **Canaanite religion** includes a whole *pantheon* of ancient Near Eastern deities. This pantheon is specifically listed in the Ugaritic texts *and* in the Hebrew Bible. It includes the gods **El, Baal,** and **Asherah** among others. **El was the king of all the Canaanite gods**.

Image 4: Ugaritic Stele of El
Dated Between 1400 – 1150 BCE

This picture of an ancient Ugaritic artifact shows how the ancient Canaanites viewed El. They drew this carving of him in stone. This artifact comes from the ancient port city of Ugarit. It shows the Canaanite god, El, sitting on his throne and being served by someone who is possibly a Canaanite king or priest. **El was imagined as a god of kings and fathers**. He was **seen as the king of the other Canaanite gods and the father of all the other gods**. In this way, El has a similar description to the God of the Bible.

However, archaeologists have discovered ancient Canaanite writings about El that portray him *very differently* than the God of the Bible. **The Canaanite El had sex with human women. He got shamefully drunk and humiliated himself at a party. El also did other typical activities that would be expected of ancient pagan deities.** Based on comparing ancient mythologies and languages, it is clear that **El** was the Canaanite version of the Sumerian god called **Anu** who came much earlier in ancient history. Furthermore, El was the Canaanite version of the later gods **Kronos** from the Greek pantheon and **Saturn** from the Roman pantheon.

Scholars have discovered these things through reading many ancient texts from different origins *outside the Bible*. These ancient texts include the Babylonian Creation Myth called *Enuma Elish* and the *Ras Shamra* Tablets. **The *Ras Shamra* Tablets contain the ancient Ugaritic mythology detailing the identities of the Canaanite gods such as El and Baal.** In the Canaanite writings, **Baal is described as the most important son of El.** El had <u>**70 sons**</u> through his wife. El's wife was a goddess called <u>**Asherah**</u>.

Baal, Asherah, and El are *all specifically mentioned* in the Hebrew Bible. The worship of El is seen as worship of the one true God of Israel. *But the worship of Baal and Asherah is strictly forbidden and condemned as idolatry.* One interesting anomaly that comes from comparing the Canaanite writings and the Bible is that the Canaanite myths *never* mention <u>**Yahweh**</u>. This is *very* strange since Yahweh is *specifically* mentioned in several ancient artifacts alongside the Canaanite goddess, **Asherah**.

Image 5: Taanach Cult Stand (references Yahweh & Asherah Together)
Dated Between 1100s – 900s BCE

For example, Image 5 shows an artifact that was recently discovered that came from ancient Israel. It is a **cult stand used for the worship of both Yahweh *and* Asherah**. It portrays Yahweh as <u>**Asherah's husband**</u>. **Yahweh is the *most* important name of the God of Israel in the Hebrew Bible**. In the Canaanite writings, Asherah is <u>**El's wife**</u>. This implies a **connection between El and Yahweh**, but this connection is *not clear*. For this reason, the origin of the Israelite God called Yahweh is a ***mystery*** that is hotly debated among ancient Near Eastern scholars to this day. Since Yahweh is *not* mentioned in the Canaanite myths, it is safe to conclude that Yahweh was *not* a Canaanite god. So, in the mind of naturalist scholars, *where* did Yahweh come from? Where was he *first* worshipped?

The Mystery of YHWH
(academically pronounced as "Yahweh")

Image 6: *Kuntillet Ajrud Shrine Inscriptions*
Dated Between 825 – 775 BCE

Image 7: *Khirbet el-Qom Burial Inscriptions*
Dated Between 750 – 700 BCE

Here you can see 2 more ancient artifacts with **inscriptions that specifically mention *both* Yahweh and Asherah together**. These inscriptions pair Yahweh and Asherah together as *husband and wife*. The picture on the left came from the ancient territory of the Sinai desert just outside of the land of Israel. This artifact dates to the time of the kings of Judah and Israel in the Bible. The ancient Hebrew writing above the picture is fragmented, but when the fragmented phrases are translated, it says:

> *"I have blessed you by YHWH of Samaria and his Asherah...I bless you by YHWH of Teman and by his Asherah...give YHWH of Teman and his ASHERAH...YHWH of Teman and his ASHERAH."*

Yahweh is associated with the ancient **Israelite city of Samaria in the north** and the ancient **Edomite city of Teman in the south**. Beneath the inscription, it appears that someone drew a picture of Yahweh and Asherah together, but this is *not directly stated* in the inscription. The picture on the right comes from a bit later in Israelite history from the **Kingdom of Judah in the southern part of the land of Israel**. It was found just **south of Jerusalem between the ancient cities of Lachish and Hebron**. This came from an ancient tomb and was a burial inscription with a handprint on it. The inscription is somewhat fragmented, but the clear part says:

> *"Uryahu the wealthy man had it written: 'Blessed be Uryahu by YHWH and from his oppressors by his Asherah he has saved him; written by Oniyahu...by his Asherah...and his Asherah.'"*

Both ancient artifacts show a clear connection between the **Israelite God, <u>Yahweh</u>**, and the **Canaanite goddess, <u>Asherah</u>**. They *strongly* imply that many Israelites viewed Asherah as Yahweh's *wife*. Archaeological discoveries like these are used by some naturalist scholars to construct their view of the Bible's God. In their theory, Yahweh was originally just **another pagan god of** *many* **in the ancient world**. But this still leaves the **mystery of Yahweh's origin**. *Who* were the first people to worship Yahweh? There are many theories from modern scholars about the correct answer to this question, but none of them have been proven. Here are the **4 most popular answers to this question about Yahweh's origin in the ancient polytheistic world**. After I discuss these 4 main theories about Yahweh's origins, I will discuss a **fifth theory among naturalist scholars that is newer**. **The first 2 of these views argue Yahweh originated <u>within the Canaanite religion</u>. The last 3 theories argue that Yahweh originated <u>outside of the Canaanite religion</u>**. These last 3 views think Yahweh came into the Israelite religion through Hebrew contact with other nations or tribes outside the land of Canaan.

In the first 2 views, Yahweh's origin is somehow *directly connected* with the Canaanite god called **<u>El</u>**. In Canaanite mythology, **El had <u>70 sons</u> who were considered members of the Canaanite pantheon**. These other gods included **Baal** from the Bible. Based on the original Hebrew language of the Biblical Text, some argue that **Yahweh was** *also* **one of the 70 sons of El**. In this view, Yahweh would be considered Baal's brother and rival for the throne of their father. This view is supported by the Canaanite myth of Baal having wars with his other brothers including **<u>Yam</u>** and **<u>Mot</u>**.

The Hebrew Bible's original language is also used to support this view. For example, we can see that **Yahweh is portrayed as a son of El in some versions of Deuteronomy 32:8-9**. The Dead Sea Scrolls are some of the *oldest* available manuscripts of the Hebrew Bible today. Deuteronomy 32:8-9 in the Dead Sea Scrolls says:

> *"When Elyon gave the nations their inheritance, when he separated the sons of Adam, he set the bounds of the people according to the number of the sons of El. So Yahweh's portion is His people; Jacob is the lot of His inheritance."*

If this interpretation is correct, the ancient Israelites would have originally viewed **Yahweh as a <u>*son of El*</u> rather than as viewing El and Yahweh as 2 names for the same deity**. This is the <u>**first theory**</u>. The main problem with this view is that it relies solely on the Bible for its premise. **Yahweh is *not* mentioned *at all* in the Canaanite texts about their pagan religion outside the Hebrew Bible**.

For this reason, some scholars reject this theory and prefer to view **Yahweh as an ancient <u>epithet</u> for El**. An epithet is basically a nickname which describes divine attributes. For example, in Greek mythology, Zeus is called the *god of thunder*. This is an *epithet*. In this <u>**second theory**</u> of Yahweh's origins, the **meaning** of Yahweh is analyzed more than the sound of the name itself. In Hebrew, the name "*Yahweh*" means "*the One Who causes to become.*" Just as Zeus is the god of thunder, **El is the One Who causes to become**, or the *One Who creates*.

Archeologists discovered an ancient Canaanite city called **Ebla** in 1964. This discovery led to many controversies in the field of Biblical Studies. **The ancient Canaanite writings found at Ebla include evidence of biblical names with reference to *El* and *Yah*.** One group of researchers *suggested* that the name *Yah* came to replace *El* in certain names. This would be a connection between the Canaanite god, El, and the shorter version of the name "Yahweh." This view seemed to hold the most promise for providing an origin of the worship of Yahweh. But it has largely been *discredited* by most scholars today. The supposed "evidence" that the researchers used to propose this connection does not hold up to strict academic scrutiny.

The **third theory** of the origin of Yahweh-worship **separates Yahweh from the Canaanite god, El**. In this third view, Yahweh was a very small, mostly *insignificant tribal deity*. He was associated with the ancient nomadic tribes who are listed as distant relatives to the ancient Israelites in the Bible. There are various versions of this theory. But ultimately, the theory argues that Yahweh was originally the family god of the **Edomites**, the **Midianites**, the **Kenites**, or possibly **other** *small tribes*. What these tribes had in common was that they *wandered around* various parts of the ancient Near East. These tribes were **nomads** who lived in **tents in the wilderness**. In this view, Yahweh's *exact* origin is unknown. But he *may* have originally gone by a **shorter form of his name** such as *Yah* or *Yahu*.

This third view is officially known as the **Kenite, Midianite,** *or* **Edomite Hypothesis**. There are a lot of different variations in this view. For example, some scholars believe that Yahweh, or *Yahuah*, was originally the name of a massive **volcano** in the ancient territory of **Anatolia**. Anatolia refers to the territory of modern-day **Turkey**, just **north of the land of Israel**. Others who embrace this theory typically agree that **Yahweh was a volcanic mountain** *or* **thunderstorm god**. However, they would contend that **Yahweh originated south of the land of Israel in the Sinai desert near Egypt**.

In most cases, this third theory about the origin of Yahweh states that **this tribal deity was originally a** *brutal* **god of war**. They say he was like *Aries* in the Greek pantheon and *Mars* in the Roman pantheon. Some scholars assert that this was the origin of the God of Israel before the Jews eventually adopted monotheism. In this view, **the Jews adopted monotheism by combining this war god with other Canaanite deities in a process of ancient syncretism**. This third view is based on a mix of content from the Bible and ancient Near Eastern archaeology. The newer, fifth view that I will discuss momentarily uses elements of this third view for support.

The **fourth theory** of the origin of Yahweh **hinges on a specific study of his Hebrew name**. The Bible contains a short form of this name which can be pronounced "*Yah*." This sound is found in the famous word "*Hallelujah*" which is usually translated as "*Praise the Lord.*" It is generally accepted among Bible scholars that the name "*Yah*" came from the name **Yahweh**. Most would argue that the name "**Yah**" is a **diminutive form** of the full name "**Yahweh**." A diminutive form refers to a nickname used to show endearment and intimacy. For example, "Mikey" is the diminutive form of the full name "Michael." Based on where it is found in the original language of the Bible, many argue that "**Yah**" is a **more personal, endearing call upon Yahweh**. However, some scholars would argue that the full name, "Yahweh," came from the shorter form, "*Yah*."

The name "*Yah*" can be found **49 times** in the Hebrew Bible. It's **first occurrence is in Exodus chapter 15**. Many scholars believe this chapter is either the **oldest** or *one of the oldest* writings in the Bible. The name can be found here in **Exodus 15:2**. When translated from the original language, this verse reads:

> "*Yah is my strength and song, and he has become my liberation: he is my El, and I will prepare him a home; my father's Elohim, and I will lift him up.*"

In English, this short name of Yahweh is spelled *Y-A-H*. But the pronunciation is "*Yah*" or "*EE-AH*." In this fourth view, we must understand a brief background about the **evolution of the Mesopotamian religion from the ancient Sumerians**. The Sumerian pantheon of gods shifted over hundreds of years as their political situation changed. Originally, the head of their pantheon was a god called **An** or **Anu**. Anu had 2 sons named **Enlil** and **Enki**. **The attributes of these 2 gods were later combined into a Hittite or Hurrian god called *Ea***. This name is spelled *E-A*, but it could be *pronounced* as either *"EE," "AY,"* or *"EE-AH."*

In this theory of the origin of Yahweh, this Mesopotamian god's name is pronounced as *"EE-AH"* or <u>*Yah*</u>. This is the origin of the Israelite God, Yahweh, in his most ancient form. In Mesopotamian mythology, *Yah* was the **creator of mankind**. The culture of ancient Sumer spread across the ancient Near East to the lands of the **Hittites and Canaanites**. This is where the **Mesopotamian god** *Ea* or *Yah* came to be worshipped along with other gods. This is the fourth theory of the origin of Yahweh.

In November 2020, a professor at New York University named **Dr. Daniel E. Fleming** published a new academic treatise called ***Yahweh Before Israel: Glimpses of History in a Divine Name***. In this book, Fleming carefully re-traces archaeological evidence, biblical content, and naturalist theories I have referenced here—particularly the third view relating to the Midianite Hypothesis—to construct a **new theory of the origin of Yahweh**. This is the **fifth theory** I will describe. Fleming begins his argument with an in-depth look at archeological findings from ancient Egypt. With a team of other Egyptologists and related researchers, he examines the remains of the ancient Egyptian temples of **Soleb**, **Amarah-West**, and **Medinet Habu**. I will discuss these extremely important archeological discoveries in chapter 6 of Volume II. For now, you should know that these **Egyptian temples** refer to *someone*, or *something*, called *"Yahu."*

It is generally understood among most scholars that *"<u>Yahu</u>"* in these Egyptian temples is somehow related to *"<u>Yahweh</u>,"* the mysterious God of the Hebrew Bible. Fleming uses this understanding to craft his theory of Yahweh's origins. Using the archeological evidence and other available ancient Egyptian texts, Fleming makes a connection between this "**Yahu**" and an ancient group known to the Egyptians as the "**Shasu**." The Egyptians viewed the "Shasu" as a **broad population of nomads with different tribes that lived all around the ancient Near East**. The Shasu were found **in the north and in the south**. They were spread out throughout the land. The Egyptian temples at Soleb, Amarah-West, and Medinet Habu all refer to **multiple different groups or tribes** that lived in the "lands of Shasu." *One of the tribes or groups among the Shasu is called "Yahu."*

Using this carefully studied observation as his starting point, Fleming goes on to use the biblical text, other ancient Near Eastern texts, and other archeological discoveries to argue that the "*Yahu of Shasu-land*" was a unique tribe among the Shasu that thrived in the ancient world. Fleming argues that "Yahu" originally referred to a specific *group of people*. They were *one of the tribes* of the nomadic Shasu. They were *separate* from the group that was known as "*Israel*," and the Hebrew Bible refers to this people called "*Yahu*" or "**Yahweh**" several times. In the eyes of Fleming, the earliest historical reference to this tribe was composed in **Judges 5:11 and 5:13**, which translates:

> "At the sound of those who divide flocks among the watering places, there they shall give the righteous deeds of **YHWH**, the righteous deeds for his farmers in Israel. Then **the people of YHWH** went down to the gates…Then survivors came down to the mighty ones; **the people of YHWH** came down to me as **warriors**."

The text literally refers to *"the people of Yahweh."* This same formulation is found in Ezekiel 36:20, Zephaniah 2:10, Numbers 11:29, Numbers 16:41, 1 Samuel 2:24, 2 Samuel 1:12, 2 Samuel 6:21, and 2 Kings 9:6. Fleming argues that "**Yahweh**" originally referred to a **community of nomads** and possibly **rural inhabitants outside the cities of Canaan and Israel**. Using his research about the biblical people connected with the Kingdom of Moab and other ancient communities in South Arabia called the Sabaeans and the Qatabanians, Fleming suggests that **Yahweh was a personal god connected with a close-knit tribal people with the** *same name*. This god and this tribe, in Fleming's view, were *inseparable*. Fleming upholds that Yahweh was originally the god of a people *without kings* and *without cities*.

However, this "**Yahweh-people**" would have likely **associated their personal god with the greater gods of the cities and political entities around them**. When the political entity that was ancient Israel eventually grew in prominence, kings of Israel, such as Omri, had to accept and integrate tribes like the *"Yahu" and their gods* (with the same names) into their larger political structure based in large cities. Beginning from this point, "**Yahweh**" **evolved from the shared name of a nomadic Shasu tribe and their local deity to a competing national god of the political entity known as "Israel."** In time, Yahweh would become **equal** with the foreign, national Canaanite god called "**El**." Then Yahweh-El would become the *only* God when Jewish monotheism was born. This is Fleming's argument in his book, the fifth theory about the origin of Yahweh according to naturalist scholars.

So, *where* did Yahweh come from? The simple answer is *no one knows for sure*. Outside the Hebrew Bible, Yahweh is mostly a

mystery. Yahweh *may* have been connected with ancient Canaanite religion, but there is very little evidence to prove this. Yahweh *may* have been connected to even more ancient Mesopotamian religion, but there is also very little evidence to prove this. Most evidence outside the Bible seems to suggest that the **worship of Yahweh originated among nomads outside the land of Canaan**. This is consistent with the Bible's story. However, this vague notion leaves other details up to scholarly imaginations. What is clear from the Bible is that somehow, *Yahweh and El came to be the same God*, and this God became the *only* God of the Jewish people.

However, before Yahweh became the only God of the Jews, He somehow had a controversial history connected with the Canaanite pantheon worshipped in ancient Israel. Scholars such as **Dr. Francesca Stavrakopoulou** and archaeologists such as **Dr. Israel Finkelstein** use detailed artifact and textual analysis to support their view that there were originally **many competing groups of people who worshipped Yahweh in drastically different ways**. Most *did not* worship Yahweh as their *only* God. Instead, they worshipped Yahweh as one of many powerful gods.

Those in Israel and outside of Israel who did worship Yahweh as *the one and only God* are called **Yahwists**, and their religion is called **Yahwism**. There is much evidence to suggest that there were **multiple schools of Yahwism**. Not all Yahwists agreed about how Yahweh *should* be worshipped. **Some Yahwists worshipped Yahweh in ways that the Bible forbids**. There are **2 noteworthy examples** naturalist scholars use to support the idea that ancient Israel had competing schools of Yahwism.

First, the Bible clearly states that **Yahweh only has *one legitimate temple***, and Yahweh's Temple is in **Jerusalem**. However, archaeological evidence clearly reveals that Israelites and even later

Jews **built temples for Yahweh** *outside Jerusalem*. Archaeological findings suggest that there was a prominent **temple of Yahweh in ancient Samaria**, the capital of the Northern Kingdom of Israel. The Bible makes *no reference* to *any* such temple, and this seems to be clearly for political reasons. The Bible is pro-David and pro-Jerusalem. Ultimately, the Bible supports the Southern Kingdom of Judah over the Northern Kingdom of Israel, and the capital of Judah is **Jerusalem**.

Meanwhile, another ancient Israelite temple was somehow built at a place called **Tel Arad**. This temple dates to around 950 BCE, near the time of King Solomon. Researchers did lab tests that found traces of **cannabis, frankincense**, and **other related chemical substances** that suggests that the ancient Israelites who worshipped Yahweh at this temple used **hallucinogens** as part of their sacred services. Later, after Jerusalem was destroyed by King Nebuchadnezzar, Jewish exiles who fled to Egypt built a temple of Yahweh in **Elephantine**. Artifacts from this Elephantine temple suggest that these Jewish people also worshipped other gods in addition to Yahweh at this temple, or simply that these Jews worshipped Yahweh with pagan methods that the Bible forbids.

Second, the Bible clearly states that **Yahweh** *does not* **want to be worshipped in certain ways**. For example, the Bible *forbids* those who worship Yahweh by building *any* **idols** at all—*even if the idol is meant to represent Yahweh*. In her book, *God: An Anatomy*, Francesca Stavrakopoulou describes in detail many different passages in the Hebrew Bible that hint at or directly state the fact that some Yahwists worshipped Yahweh with special idols that represented His physical likeness. Stavrakopoulou suggests that passages such as **Psalm 27:4** should be interpreted *literally* to refer to a **beautiful idol** that was crafted to look like Yahweh as He was viewed in the minds of ancient

Israelites, such as David.

Another example of forbidden worship in the Hebrew Bible is **child-sacrifice**. The Bible is clear that Yahweh *hates* child sacrifice, and He never asks His people to sacrifice children to Him (2 Kings 23:10 and Jeremiah 19:1-7). However, there are some verses in the Bible that suggest that Yahweh allowed His people to think that He wanted them to sacrifice their children to Him at certain times. **Yahweh had convinced Abraham to sacrifice his son to Him as a holy burnt offering** (Genesis 22:1-10). Of course, in Abraham's story, *Yahweh stops him* from completing the sacrifice. The Israelite judge, Jephthah, also seemed convinced that offering to sacrifice his child to Yahweh would grant him more favor in a time of war. Unlike Abraham, **Jephthah physically sacrifices his only daughter as a burnt offering to Yahweh** (Judges 11:29-40).

Later, passages such as **Ezekiel 20:18-26** reveal that **some people among the Israelites believed that Yahweh wanted them to sacrifice their children to Him**. The Prophet Ezekiel explains that *Yahweh allowed the people to believe this as punishment for their sin and rebellion against Him*. The most shocking words are found in Ezekiel 20:25-26. After explaining how the Israelites rejected Yahweh's customs and replaced them with pagan customs, Yahweh says to them:

> "And **I <u>also</u> *gave them* customs that were *not* good and judgments by which they *could not* live**; and I pronounced them unclean because of *their gifts*, in that *they caused all their firstborn to pass through the fire so that I might make them desolate*, in order that they might know that I am YHWH.'"

These words reveal that at some point in Israelite history, **a certain school of Yahwism told their followers that Yahweh wanted them to sacrifice their firstborn children to Yahweh**. Stavrakopoulou and other naturalist scholars point to these things to argue against any unified monotheistic religion in ancient Israel. They argue that Jewish monotheism came later, but it was likely based on a specific school of Yahwism that rejected grotesque pagan practices such as child sacrifice, building expensive idols, and worshipping other gods. For naturalist scholars, all these revelations from the Bible *completely discredit* traditional Judeo-Christian beliefs about God and His people.

For those of us who **trust** the God of the Bible and believe His testimony, we must **wrestle** with these uncomfortable observations and continue to trust Jesus through it all. The name "**Israel**" means "**He Wrestles with El / God**." If we want the blessing, we must continually wrestle with God, facing the difficult questions and challenges that naturalist scholars present (Genesis 32:24-30).

Remember, the naturalist worldview approaches the Bible as an ancient mythological text. The true origin of the worship of Yahweh in the ancient world remains a mystery. None of the 5 theories I discussed have ever been proven, and archeological evidence outside the Bible scarcely mentions the name *Yahweh* at all. But this lack of clarity about the origin of Israel's Yahweh-worship does not persuade anyone with the naturalist worldview to embrace a traditional Judeo-Christian perspective on the Bible. Instead, naturalist scholars focus on the pagan associations with Yahweh's origins to deny the credibility of the Bible's message.

Israelite Henotheism Affirming Naturalist Worldview

The Bible alone makes it clear that the ancient Hebrews were *not strict monotheists*. The popular religion of ancient Canaan was the same religion of ancient Israel: **polytheism**. Based on the text of the Bible and other ancient sources, it seems that *exclusive* **Israelite worship of Yahweh began as a cult which grew in popularity over time**. On this basis, it is logical to conclude that the ancient Israelites were *henotheistic*. **Henotheism** is the belief that many gods exist, but only *one* **God** is *greater* **than all others and should be worshipped as such**.

It is obvious even based on the Bible's testimony that ancient Israelites worshipped *many* gods for most of the Old Testament story. On this basis, scholars today debate how the ancient Jews moved **from polytheism to henotheism**, and **then to monotheism** before the time of Jesus Christ. Scholars with the naturalist worldview see most ancient religions as the product of **evolution**. They believe that somehow, the Jews combined the Canaanite god, El, with Yahweh and possibly other gods from the ancient Near East. They created *one new god in the image of many older gods*. Then they **banned the worship of *all* the old gods** and lifted up **Yahweh as the One true God with** *many* **different titles**.

All these subjects that I have discussed so far come together to form the popular, secular view of the Old Testament today. This text is seen as an ancient document which presents archaic views of the world. It is an example of the savage paganism of the ancient world. In this sense, the Old Testament is the Hebrew version of Homer's *Iliad*. The main difference is that the Hebrew religion is still practiced in its evolved forms today, and the Greek religion has gone extinct.

Because of **archaeological evidence**, scholars are forced to admit that some **actual history is recorded in the Old Testament**. But naturalism forces them to use their skills of analysis to *"de-mythicize"* the ancient text to distinguish historical facts from the grand legends of the ancient Hebrews. In the naturalist worldview, Moses and other famous Bible characters such as David were never the authors of the Old Testament. Instead, this colorful text was a conglomeration of many ancient writings which all came from the **ancient Hebrew tribal traditions**. These traditions were **mixed** with the Sumerian, Egyptian, and Canaanite cultures. They evolved from folktales to written literature.

Finally, this view of the Bible firmly rejects the idea that the Old Testament is God's message to humanity. Instead, the Old Testament is a story of ancient people, their culture, and their evolving beliefs about the nature of reality. This is how the Bible is viewed in public schools and universities today. **They come to these conclusions about the Bible using the worldviews of <u>humanism</u> and <u>naturalism</u>**.

The Mythicist Vs. Historicist Perspectives on the Bible

If you are a Jew or a Christian reading this book, you may feel challenged or discouraged by this chapter about how modern scholars view the Bible. If this is the case, then I want to offer you some encouragement and an important note about recent changes in the field of biblical studies. Within the last 200 years or so, the secular view of the Bible has changed *dramatically*. This happened based on many discoveries in the important historical field of **archaeology**.

There was a time in the past few hundred years when some scholars concluded that the *entire* Bible was a *complete work of fiction with no historical accuracy in it <u>at all</u>*. Some people even argued that the Bible was written by people who lived in the time of the Roman Empire, or by Jews in Medieval Europe. Based on these now-outdated theories, some scholars were able to destroy many people's faith and discredit the Bible's authenticity in history.

This now-outdated view of the Bible is called the **Mythicist** perspective. Essentially, this perspective states that the stories and characters of the Bible are *completely fiction* and have *no element of historical fact in them at all*. The Mythicists argue that there was *never* any distinct group of people called Israel. They argue that there was *never* any man named Abraham or Moses or *even* David. Regarding the New Testament, they argue that there was *never* any man named Jesus of Nazareth.

Instead, the Mythicists propose an **alternative theory for the origins of the Bible's content**. They say that both the stories of Moses leading to **Judaism** and the stories of Jesus leading to **Christianity** were **recent fabrications rooted in ancient Egyptian mystery religion**. This ancient mystery religion revolved around the cult of the Egyptian gods **Osiris** and **Horus**. According to the Mythicist theory, this mystery religion was adapted over the years during the rise of the ancient Greek and Roman Empires.

These Mythicists used to argue that there was *no such thing* as *any* of the gods of the Bible. They claimed that there was *never any god called Yahweh, El, Baal, Asherah, Dagon,* or *any other god* listed in the Bible. **These views of the Mythicist perspective were mostly discredited and disproven with recent archaeological discoveries.** These discoveries forced scholars to accept the reality of the Bible's **legitimacy** as an ancient text.

Unfortunately, because of massive ignorance, the Mythicist perspective on the Bible is *still* spread today in popular culture. It is presented clearly in so-called *"academic"* documentaries such as the

Zeitgeist movie that was released in 2007. Beware such documentaries and beware *any* source that suggests that the Bible is completely based on myths and has no historical reality whatsoever. Even the most prominent naturalist Bible scholars, such as those I listed previously, know that the Bible has roots in actual history. The Bible is *not* founded on myths. It is *not* a comic book or a fiction novel. Nevertheless, most of the naturalist scholars I have listed in this chapter would agree with the Mythicist perspective that figures such as Abraham and Moses were characters *mostly* based on ancient legends.

The most recent archaeological discoveries have proven that the Bible is an ancient text based on historical events of the ancient Near East. This is called the **Historicist** perspective on the Bible. According to this perspective, **the stories and characters of the Bible are, *to a greater or lesser degree,* based on historical facts**. The Bible's contents are all somehow connected to actual events that took place in world history. **Most serious Bible scholars today are Historicists, *even if* they are also naturalists**.

It is important to realize that there are *many* different types of people who embrace the Historicist perspective. For example, **an atheist Historicist agrees that there was an ancient people called "Israel" and that they had kings such as Omri, Josiah, and Hezekiah.** *Some* of them even agree that there really was a King David and Solomon—although many naturalist scholars deny that David and Solomon existed as they are described in the Bible. But **an atheist Historicist will have a naturalist worldview**. On that basis, they will deny *any* supernatural occurrences or "miracles" that are mentioned in the Bible. But a Christian Historicist will argue that *all the miracles* listed in the Bible happened *exactly* as they are written. **Christian Historicists believe the God of the Bible is real *and* still**

active today.

The main unifying factor about *all* Historicists is that they support the fact that the people mentioned in the Bible were, indeed, **real people in the history of the world**. This includes the people of **Israel**, sometimes **Moses** (depending on the scholar), usually **David** (depending on the scholar, *although many naturalists would argue his true story is unknown and the Bible's story is merely a politically contrived legend*), and **Jesus** in the New Testament. **A Mythicist thinks that *everything* in the Bible is a fairytale with no basis in real history. A Historicist thinks the stories in the Bible may *or* may not be true**. But they *also* think the people of the Bible were, *more or less*, actual historical figures who lived and died on this planet.

Archaeological discoveries have largely disproven *and* discredited the Mythicist perspective on the Bible. Most naturalist scholars today who *carefully* study the Bible agree that it does have *some* myths in it. However, it was ***not fabricated*** as a book of myths without ties to actual human history.

Archaeology's Importance in Studying the Bible

Here is a brief overview of the archaeological evidence which overwhelmingly supports the historicity of the Hebrew Bible. The people of Israel are specifically mentioned in ancient Egyptian sources and in other ancient Near Eastern sources outside the Bible. Furthermore, other peoples of the Bible such as the Midianites, Moabites, and Edomites are also mentioned in these ancient sources.

The discovery of the ancient port city of **Ugarit** proved the legitimacy of the ancient Canaanite religion. Before this major archeological discovery, many scholars thought that the Canaanite religion discussed in the Bible was a myth. The discovery of the ancient civilization and city of **Sumer** was another crucial event. Sumer shows a strong compatibility with the Bible's land of **Shinar**. In the ancient city of Sumer, they found evidence of mountain-like temples called **ziggurats**. These ziggurats verify the idea behind the story of the **Tower of Babel**.

Another example of archeology proving the nonfiction background of the Old Testament is the mention of the **house of David** in an ancient writing. David's royal line is mentioned as being defeated by another ancient Near Eastern king. This shows that there was a man named David and that he had a royal dynasty among the people of Israel and their land. Also, the city of Ugarit thoroughly describes the Canaanite god called **El**. As I stated previously, El is the Hebrew name of God and the root of the Hebrew word *Elohim*. **This is one of the most popular names of God in the Bible.**

Furthermore, an Egyptian and a Moabite source *both* mention a God called **Yahweh**. In these sources, this *Yahweh* is directly connected with a group of people called **Israelites**. Finally, **many different ancient historians** testified to the existence of the **Jewish people** and their unique identity in the ancient world. Roman historians mention the Jewish people frequently because the Roman Empire had a lot of trouble with them. The Jewish historians **Philo** and **Josephus** discuss specific events in the history of the Jewish people. Most of these events are *also* recorded in the Hebrew Bible. But these Jewish historians add details to these stories. They also expand upon what happened to the Jewish people *after* the Hebrew Bible's narrative ends.

These ancient Roman and Jewish sources show that the Jews were a distinct group of people for *at least* **the past 2,000 years.** Even 500 years *earlier* than *that* time, **Persian sources** show that the Jews existed as a unique culture. Based on these things, we see that there really were a group of people called the **Israelites**, or **Hebrews**. Modern Jews can trace their lineage back to these ancient origins. **All of this demonstrates that the Bible has a rich historical background that intersects with most of Western history going all the way back to the ancient Egyptian Empire**—*around 4,000 years ago*.

I encourage you to embrace a Historicist perspective on the Hebrew Bible. This is the perspective that I will use in this series. Here I have given you a brief overview of major archaeological evidence used to support the real history in the Hebrew Bible. In Volume II of this series, I discuss more specific examples of this evidence. But for now, you can see that the Historicist perspective on the Bible is *most* compatible with modern scholarship. This is true regardless of your religious background. Now we will turn from examining the naturalist worldview of the Bible to focus on the worldview of **Judaism**.

Chapter 4
The Worldview of Judaism

Five Types of Judaism

As I stated previously, both Christianity and Islam are the most popular religions of the modern world. But these two religions ultimately derived from ancient Judaism. This is somewhat ironic since Judaism is now one of the least popular religions in the world. But even within the religion of Judaism itself, there is a wide variety of differing traditions and beliefs. There are many different types of Judaism among those who practice it today. I have listed 5 main types of modern Judaism here:

1. **Rabbinic** (*Rabbi-Centered*) Judaism — **most common and widely-recognized.**

2. **Reformed** (*Culture-Centered*; Rabbinic) Judaism

3. **Conservative** (*Tradition-Centered*; Rabbinic) Judaism

4. **Karaite** (*Scripture-Centered*; **NOT Rabbinic**) Judaism

5. **Messianic** (*Yeshua-Centered*; **Rabbinic Influence Varies**) Judaism

There is one main question which leads to these 5 divergent

forms of Judaism. This question is: "**Who has the central religious authority in the Jewish faith?**" Different answers to this question have produced different forms of Judaism.

The most popular and probably the most dedicated form of modern Judaism is Rabbinic Judaism. Rabbinic Jews are also called orthodox or ultraorthodox Jews. They are sometimes also referred to as Hasidic Jews. In Rabbinic Judaism, the central religious authority belongs to the rabbis. Ancient rabbis hold more authority than modern rabbis. But modern rabbis still debate among themselves to determine the meanings and interpretations of the Hebrew Bible.

The purpose of these interpretations is to find the right ways to apply the Bible's teachings to their lives. Due to modern technological developments and cultural differences among Jews today, this task can be challenging. In Rabbinic Judaism, having the right interpretation of the Bible is extremely important. The right interpretation is one that follows the oral tradition of the community of rabbis throughout history. This lens used to view the Bible in Rabbinic Judaism is more important than the text itself.

An example of this comes from God's commandment to the Israelites in Exodus 23:19. This verse says: "**Do not boil a young goat in its mother's milk.**" This commandment is repeated in Exodus 34:26 and Deuteronomy 14:21. The literal meaning of this commandment is simple: if you have a young goat and its mother, do not use the mother's milk to boil or cook the young goat. This commandment likely spoke against ancient pagan practices from the Canaanite religion. But the rabbis in more recent times came up with a new and more acceptable interpretation for this commandment. Their interpretation is: "*Do not eat meat and milk together.*" This interpretation forms the basis for a major kosher law in Rabbinic Judaism.

In Rabbinic Judaism, the rabbis ultimately determine what God is saying to His people in the Bible. It is sinful in the eyes of Rabbinic Judaism to disagree with an interpretation of the rabbis unless you are a rabbi. Furthermore, any disagreement in Rabbinic Judaism must support the oral traditions of other ancient rabbis. In Rabbinic Judaism, the oral tradition is more important than the written Law of Moses.

The Legacy of Rabbinic Judaism

The other two most popular types of Judaism are politically opposite denominations. These denominations are Reformed and Conservative Judaism. Both of these types of Judaism emerged from the background of Rabbinic Judaism. They both rely heavily on Rabbinic Judaism for their belief systems. The difference is that Reformed and Conservative Judaism are more lenient and culturally flexible in their forms of practice.

Conservative Judaism emphasizes the central authority of tradition. Their tradition is connected to the ancient rabbis or sages. On the other hand, Reformed Judaism is culture-centered. It takes a very liberal approach to the Jewish faith. Reformed Judaism can be so lenient that even belief in God is optional, although this extreme is rare. Reformed and Conservative Judaism tend to emphasize the importance of the Jewish culture and people. These versions of Judaism focus on what it means to be a Jew today more than the text or ancient religion of the Hebrew Bible.

Sola Scriptura Jews

The last 2 forms of Judaism are Karaite and Messianic Judaism. I listed these 2 last because many Jews within the Rabbinic tradition would claim that Karaite and Messianic Jews are not true followers of Judaism. They would present these last 2 groups as comparable to heretics of the true Jewish faith.

Contrarily, Karaite and Messianic Jews view themselves as proponents of the true Jewish faith. Each of them would say that all other Jews in the Rabbinic background have missed something. With that said, it is important to know that Karaite and Messianic Judaism come from very different origins. Karaite and Messianic Jews disagree with each other just as much as they disagree with the Rabbinic forms of Judaism.

Karaite Judaism has a rich history which goes back into medieval times and beforehand. The word "Karaite" comes from the Hebrew word "qara" which means "to read" or "to proclaim." It refers to Jews who reject the supreme authority of the Rabbinic oral traditions. Instead of Rabbinic authority, Karaite Jews seek the literal interpretation of the Hebrew Bible.

Karaite Jews share the same Bible and much of the same background as the Rabbinic Jews. Like the Rabbinic Jews, the Karaite Jews reject the New Testament as part of the Bible. They do not believe that Jesus was the Jewish Messiah. Unlike Rabbinic Jews, Karaite Jews believe that only the Hebrew Bible is the true message of God to His people. Karaite Jews believe that the Holy Scripture should have central religious authority to determine Jewish faith and practice.

As a result, Karaite and Rabbinic Jews have had conflict with each other. They have rejected each other as misguided forms of true Judaism since ancient times. However, some Karaite Jews believe that Jesus was a Karaite Jew and a faithful proponent of the Karaite religion. Nehemia Gordon is a prominent Karaite Jewish scholar who embraces this perspective. These Karaite Jews would say that Jesus was falsely accused and condemned by the Rabbinic Jews of ancient times. In that sense, some Karaite Jews would view Jesus as a prophet; but they would not say he is the Messiah.

Contrarily, Rabbinic Judaism typically associates Jesus with an ancient Hebrew man named Yeshu. Yeshu is mentioned in writings about ancient Rabbinic oral traditions. According to this tradition, Yeshu was the product of a Roman solider raping a woman named Miriam. Miriam is the Hebrew version of the name "Mary." In this Rabbinic story, Miriam covered up the shame of her rape by telling others that Yeshu was a miracle from God and that she was still a virgin. While growing up in Egypt with his family, Yeshu learned the secret arts of Egyptian sorcery. When Yeshu came back to the land of Israel, he used this witchcraft to perform many miracles. Then, he was crucified by the Jewish leaders during the first century CE for trying to lead a rebellion against the Roman Empire. At its most negative extreme, this is the Rabbinic view of Jesus.

Jewish Responses to Jesus

Jews throughout history have typically responded to Christianity by viewing Jesus in two different ways. Some proclaim Jesus as a faithful devotee to their religion. Others say He was a wicked Man Who was worthy of the death that He received. It is at this point where Messianic Jews stand apart from the rest. Unlike all other Jews, Messianic Jews believe that Jesus of Nazareth is the Jewish Messiah.

Messianic Jews embrace the oral and cultural traditions of every other form of Judaism with varying degrees of influence. Furthermore, different Messianic Jews may disagree about different Jewish traditions and practices. But all Messianic Jews agree that

Jesus is the Messiah of the Jewish people. Messianic Jews refer to Jesus by His Aramaic Name since Aramaic was the language spoken by Jews during the First Century. Jesus' Aramaic Name is "Yeshua."

Some Messianic Jews would argue that their religion goes back to the time of the first century under different names and often in secrecy. This happened because of the tragic fact that Messianic Jews were doubly persecuted for their faith. In the earliest times, the Jewish people who rejected Jesus persecuted the Messianic Jews for accepting Jesus. Then, after Christianity became a major world religion and culturally separated from Judaism, Christians began persecuting Jews.

Christians persecuted all Jewish people for embracing Jewish culture and tradition. Sadly, Messianic Jews were caught in the middle of this persecution. They were rejected by their own people and by foreign people who agreed that Jesus is their Messiah. Jews want Messianic Jews to give up Jesus, but Christians want Messianic Jews to give up Judaism. Despite their difficult position in the middle, Messianic Jews have existed in history. But they have usually had to become more like other Jews or Christians to avoid persecution.

Some see modern Messianic Judaism going all the way back to the First Century. But others see the origin of today's Messianic Judaism in the 1970s. The modern Messianic Movement in Judaism grew out of the 1970s Jesus Movement. A group of Jews studied the person of Jesus Christ as a real Jewish man from the first century CE. By doing this, they came to believe that Jesus was indeed the true Messiah of the Jews. However, they also realized Western culture outside of Judaism tended to take away Jesus' Jewishness.

Outside of Judaism, the world typically viewed Jesus as anti-Jewish culture. Messianic Jews sought to change this stereotype by studying Jesus in the context of the ancient Jewish roots of the First Century. Messianic Jews accept the writings of the New Testament as part of the Bible, but they call it the New Covenant. Instead of attending churches, they attend synagogues. They reject many traditions of Christianity which are rooted in pagan influences from the Roman Empire.

Beside Messianic Judaism, all other forms of Judaism agree that the true Messiah of Israel has not come yet. But they look forward to a day when he will come and bring peace to the whole world. Despite this major area of disagreement between Messianic Jews and all other Jews, Messianic Jews agree with the main view of the Hebrew Bible in Judaism.

Rabbinic Judaism Vs. The Israelite Religion

Once again, I must emphasize that the most popular and the most identifiable form of Judaism today is Rabbinic Judaism. However, I must also mention that Rabbinic Judaism is not the same religion that the Israelites practiced in the Hebrew Bible. The Israelite religion required 2 key elements that are missing from all forms of modern Judaism. The first of these elements is the Holy Temple of God in Jerusalem. The second is the offering of animal sacrifices by the chosen priesthood of Moses' brother, Aaron.

Using their oral traditions, Rabbinic Judaism has replaced the Temple and animal sacrifices with different forms of practice. They host community meetings at synagogues, they read the Torah, and they practice good works along with prayer to repent from sin. In this way, Rabbinic Judaism sees itself as a direct and pure continuation of the religion of the Israelites in the Hebrew Bible. Rabbinic Jews are mainly focused with how ancient rabbis interpreted the Bible. They place oral tradition above textual authority for determining God's message to them today.

The Bible (TaNaK) in the Worldview of Judaism

All types of Judaism would agree that it is an insult to call their Bible "the Old Testament." In the eyes of most forms of Judaism, the Old Testament is their only testament. The whole Jewish Bible includes only the books of the Christian Old Testament. For this reason, Jews prefer to call their Bible by two names: the Hebrew Bible and the TaNaK.

Jews view their Bible as containing three main parts: the Torah, the Nevi'im, and the Ketuvim. These three parts form the acronym T-N-K which is pronounced as "TaNaK." Torah is the Hebrew word which English usually translates as "Law." The Torah refers to the first five books of the Old Testament. Nevi'im is the Hebrew word meaning "Prophets." This refers to most of the other narrative books in the TaNaK. The books of the Nevi'im tell the history of the people of Israel in their Promised Land. Ketuvim is the Hebrew word for "Writings." This refers to the remaining books of poetry and wisdom literature in the TaNaK. Two examples of these books are Proverbs and Psalms.

The TaNaK contains the same content as the Christian Old Testament, but it is different in the way that it presents this content to the reader. For example, the TaNaK uses a slightly different arrangement of chapter and verse markings to references its sentences in the text. The TaNaK's version of the Book of Psalms is exactly one verse off from the Book of Psalms in the Old Testament. Also, the order of the books in the Bible is different in the TaNaK than it is in the Old Testament. While the Old Testament ends with the

Book of Malachi, the TaNaK ends with the Books of Chronicles. Moreover, the Old Testament has two books which form the story of Chronicles, but this is only one book in the TaNaK.

THE BOOKS OF THE OLD TESTAMENT

	PAGE	CHAPS.		PAGE	CHAPS.		PAGE	CHAPS.
GENESIS	7	50	2 Chronicles	348	36	Daniel	638	12
Exodus	49	40	Ezra	377	10	Hosea	651	14
Leviticus	84	27	Nehemiah	385	13	Joel	656	3
Numbers	110	36	Esther	397	10	Amos	659	9
Deuteronomy	147	34	Job	404	42	Obadiah	663	1
Joshua	177	24	Psalms	425	150	Jonah	664	4
Judges	198	21	Proverbs	478	31	Micah	666	7
Ruth	219	4	Ecclesiastes	496	12	Nahum	669	3
1 Samuel	222	31	Song of Solomon	502	8	Habakkuk	671	3
2 Samuel	249	24	Isaiah	505	66	Zephaniah	673	3
1 Kings	272	22	Jeremiah	546	52	Haggai	674	2
2 Kings	298	25	Lamentations	592	5	Zechariah	676	14
1 Chronicles	323	29	Ezekiel	596	48	Malachi	683	4

Image 8: *The Bible's Table of Contents in a KJV Bible*

Books of the TA-NA-KH
The Testament of our Forefathers

TORAH *The Law of Moses*		NEVIIM *The Prophets*		KETUVIM *The Writings*	
Genesis	1	Joshua	208	Psalms	
Exodus	55	Judges	233	Proverbs	
Leviticus	97	1 Samuel	258	Job	
Numbers	128	2 Samuel	291		
Deuteronomy	170	1 Kings	319	Song of Songs	
		2 Kings	351	Ruth	
				Lamentations	
		Isaiah	382	Ecclesiastes	
		Jeremiah	447	Esther	
		Ezekiel	513		
		Hosea	564	Daniel	
		Joel	574	Ezra	
		Amos	578	Nehemiah	
		Obadiah	586	1 Chronicles	
		Jonah	588	2 Chronicles	
		Micah	590		
		Nahum	596		
		Habakkuk	599		
		Zephaniah	602		
		Haggai	605		
		Zechariah	607		
		Malachi	617		

Image 9: *The Bible's Table of Contents in a TLV Bible*

Using Images 8 & 9, you can compare the differences between the book order of the Old Testament and the book order of the TaNaK. The picture on the top is scanned from my copy of the King James

Version of the Bible. It shows the table of contents for the Old Testament's order of books. But the picture on the bottom is scanned from my copy of the Tree of Life Version, a Messianic Jewish version of the Bible. This version includes the books of the Hebrew Bible in the traditional Jewish order used in the TaNaK. Here is the list of specific books in the Christian Old Testament that have a different order in the TaNaK:

- Ruth
- 1 & 2 Chronicles
- Ezra
- Nehemiah
- Esther
- Job
- Psalms
- Proverbs
- Ecclesiastes
- Song of Solomon
- Lamentations
- Daniel

The Supremacy of the Torah

There is one last major point we need to address regarding how the Bible is viewed in Judaism. This relates to the Jewish understanding of the Torah or the first five books of the Bible. These books are Genesis, Exodus, Leviticus, Numbers, and Deuteronomy. While this is not necessarily stated directly, it is inherently understood within most forms of Judaism that the Torah is the most sacred and most significant part of the TaNaK. In this sense, it is implicitly understood that the Torah is more inspired than the rest of the Bible in the Jewish worldview. It is true that everything else in the story of the Hebrew Bible points back to the Torah. In this way, the Torah is absolutely foundational for the rest of the narrative of the Hebrew Bible.

After the Book of Deuteronomy, the rest of the Hebrew Bible always points the reader back to the content of the Torah. The Torah is also referred to as the Pentateuch. This word means "five scrolls." Jewish synagogues all over the world contain a copy of the Torah in the form of a giant scroll. These scrolls are decorated with fancy cloth and written in a stylish font. The scroll of the Torah is treated with physical sacredness. Sometimes, this Scroll is paraded around the synagogues at Jewish services. When it is not in use for weekly readings led by a rabbi, the Torah Scroll is stored safely in a special cabinet behind the pulpit.

The five books of the Torah are traditionally called the Books of Moses because Moses was originally viewed as the author of this whole text. This special attention to the books of Moses is unique to Judaism. However, it is key to understanding the modern Jewish view of the Hebrew Bible.

Chapter 5
The Worldview of Christianity

The Old Testament in the Worldview of Christianity

Most of the Western world refers to the Hebrew Bible as the Old Testament. The reason for this is due to the long yet tragic history of Christendom. Christendom refers to the absolute rule of the Christian Church in the politics. This was the bleak reality of European government for the period of one thousand years between 500 and 1500 CE.

During this timeframe and a little bit beforehand, Christians began to persecute Jews and demonize them as the source of all evil in the world. This led to cycles of intense Jewish persecution all over the different countries in Europe. These cycles of Jewish persecution ultimately culminated in the Holocaust during World War II.

History shows that despite their common origins, Christianity became more popular than Judaism in a short period of time. There were two factors which caused Jews and Christians to rapidly disassociate with each other. First, the culture of the Christian religion shifted from Judaic to Greco-Roman. Second, the social center of the Christian religion moved to the city of ancient Rome. This happened as a result of both intense persecution from Jews and increased missionary activity among the earliest Christian people.

Jews persecuted early Christians as heretics of their religion. Sadly, this led to early Christians developing a hatred for Jews, especially after the Christian religion came to be dominated by non-

Jewish people. Many non-Jewish people already didn't like Jews, so their natural anti-Semitism became self-justified by the Jewish rejection of Jesus. Consequently, when Christianity became popular, it began to separate itself completely from its Jewish roots. Furthermore, it condemned the Jewish people as an illegitimate group that God rejected for their rejection of Jesus as the Messiah.

The term "Christ" is the Greek word used to describe the Messiah. This shift in language is itself evidence of the cultural shift in early Christianity. Part of the early separation between Christians and Jews was in the way that Christians came to collect a new group of sacred writings for themselves. These are the writings that became the New Testament.

Christians embraced the Hebrew Bible as a necessary explanation of the history of their faith. But they slowly made a separation between the writings of the Hebrew Bible and their early Christian writings. These early Christian writings found in the New Testament provide the Christian interpretations of the Hebrew Bible. This eventually led to Christians having a Bible with two testaments. The Hebrew Bible became known as the "Old" Testament, and the Christian writings became known as the "New" Testament.

The first Christian Bible translator to implement this system of titles was Saint Jerome. He did this after Christianity was legalized and standardized in the Roman Empire. Within the New Testament writings, there is a reference to an old and a new covenant. But the first main Latin translation of the Christian Bible used the term "Testament" as a further way of distancing the Christian religion from Judaism.

A covenant refers to a mutually beneficial partnership between two people. On the other hand, a testament refers to a document containing the last wishes of someone who has died. A testament explains who will inherit the property of a dead person. This method of labeling parts of the Bible was a way for later Christians to denounce the Jewish religion as a heresy. The Jews had an "old" testament, but Christians had the newest one.

As a result of these things, Christians view the Hebrew Bible as "Part One" of their Bible. Their Bible is not complete without the second and greater-emphasized part of their sacred literature: the New Testament. Unlike Jews, Christians do not place any special emphasis on the Pentateuch. In fact, many Christians view the first five books of their Bible as legalistic and primeval. Christians tend to view the whole Old Testament as an example of rigid legalism and gracelessness.

Why Christians Haven't Rejected the Old Testament

Christians cannot deny the importance of the Old Testament text despite its difficulties when read together with their New Testament. When Christians read the Old Testament, they typically place a heavy emphasis on the Messianic prophecies. They see the whole Hebrew Bible as a testimony that points directly to Jesus Christ. For this reason, Christians could never truly forsake the Old Testament even if they implicitly diminish its importance in their minds.

Unfortunately, many Christians take the Old Testament for granted. It is typically portrayed as a time of darkness before God's grace and love was revealed to the world. It is viewed as a time of sin, death, and the rule of the Law of Moses. Christians usually view the Law of Moses as a strict and condemning code of conduct that no human being could ever obey. As a result, Christians say that Jesus came to perfectly obey the Law of Moses and to bring the New Covenant of God's grace and mercy to the whole world. Christians would say that God did this for the Jews and all other nations on Earth.

Christians typically explain the warfare and brutality in the Old Testament as the result of people being under sin and the Law of Moses. Yet by way of contradiction, they historically used the holy wars described in the Old Testament as justification for them to participate in European wars. Many political revolutions throughout Western history have been justified by Christians because of the Old Testament story of the Israelites going to war against the Canaanites. Even though Jesus commanded His disciples to love their enemies (see Matthew 5:38-48), Christians typically tend to use the Old Testament to justify ideals of nationalism within different Western countries.

Please understand that I am speaking about tendencies of Christianity in Western history right now. I am not saying that all Christians have universally behaved this way or thought this way. I am merely exposing an unfortunate trend in the history of Christian culture.

God's Word: A Lesser Revelation?

While this is usually not directly stated, Christians tend to speak about the Hebrew Bible as a lesser revelation from God. He gave this revelation to His people before the greater revelation of the New Testament. This is not an official stance of the Christian religion at all. If any Christian ever taught this view directly, they would be rebuked by other Christians for doing so. Christians are taught to value the Old Testament as an essential part of their Bible. But they still tend to refer to it in the same way that a computer programmer would refer to an older software or an outdated operating system.

In all forms of Christianity, there is a unifying belief that the Bible's Old and New Testaments form the Word of God. They argue that the Bible is God's specific message to all humanity. They would say that when a person reads the Bible, they are reading the Words of God Himself. For this reason, many Christians use the phrase "the Word of God" as a synonym for their Bible.

In the Christian perspective, the Word of God refers to the most important book in the world: The Bible. The first part of this book is the Old Testament. Christians are generally united in their view that the Bible is the Word of God. But they are divided in their views about how people should interpret what is written in the Bible today. Different types of Christianity hold to different views of the Old Testament.

Old Testament Interpretations in Christianity

Just as there are many denominations of the Jewish religion, there are many different denominations of the Christian religion. The three main denominations of the Christian faith are: the Catholic Church, the Eastern Orthodox Church, and the Protestant Church. Within those three main branches of Christianity, there are many smaller denominations which disagree about certain details of how to interpret the Bible. This is true especially within the Protestant Church. Here are five main opposing views among Christians today.

First, Catholics and Protestants have historically had different levels of reverence for the Bible. Protestants have typically placed more authority and value on the Bible and have popularized it as the Word of God. But Catholics see it as very important sacred literature without elevating it above other traditions of the Western Church.

Among Protestants, there are many different views of the Old

Testament today. Some of these views focus on how to translate or give commentary on the meanings of the Bible in its ancient context. There are some Christians who support a group method of interpreting the text. But others would firmly argue that an individual and personalized method of interpreting the Bible is better. In a personalized interpretation, each individual Christian can apply the meaning of the text to their own lives.

Some Christians hold to a conservative view of the Bible. They would firmly support the idea that the Bible was written by Moses, David, and the other famous individuals mentioned in its text. Other Christians still believe the testimony of the Bible to greater or lesser degrees. But they argue for a liberal or progressive view of the Bible's authorship. This view is based on the recent scholarly studies of textual criticism that I mentioned in the third chapter of this volume.

Some Christians firmly believe that every story in the Bible should be interpreted literally as an actual historical event. Other Christians believe that while some stories in the Bible were actual historical events, other stories were not meant to be understood as actual history. Some Christians would argue that certain content in the Old Testament are allegories to teach deep spiritual lessons in the form of parables.

For example, some Christians see the story of Adam and Eve in the Garden of Eden as a literal historical event. They would say that there really was a place on this Earth called the Garden of Eden. The first human being was named Adam and his wife was named Eve. They would argue that all human beings can trace their family lines all the way back to Adam and Eve. But other Christians would see the story of Adam and Eve as a myth. They would say God included this in the Bible for the sake of teaching people a lesson about their lives, not to give knowledge about actual historical events. These

Christians do not believe there ever was a real person named Adam or Eve.

Some Christians argue that human beings came from the natural process of evolution as explained in the modern science of biology. Some Christians believe that God created the Earth in seven literal days. But others believe that God used the big bang and the long process of evolution to create the whole world. Many of these drastically different interpretations of the Bible focus on the first book of the Old Testament: Genesis.

The study of how people interpret the Bible is called hermeneutics. Christian schools and universities teach different types of hermeneutics based on their unique backgrounds. Regardless of all these diverse worldviews of the Bible among Christians, Christianity in general is united in their acceptance of the fact that the Old Testament is part of their Holy Bible. Christians believe that if any person reads the Old Testament, God will use this text to reveal Himself to them.

Chapter 6

How Other Worldviews Read the Bible

The Bible in the Worldview of Blended Beliefs

It is human nature for all of us to think in shallow ways about those who are different from us. We are typically very good at labeling others and assuming we know everything about them even if we have never met them or talked to them before. But the truth is, the people in this world are so unique and complex in their individuality that we can never know everything about even a single person, let alone a whole group of people.

There is no way that I could ever cover all the unique worldviews that are used to interpret the Bible. But this first volume is meant to give you a decent summary of major worldviews that are used to read the Bible today. The last major worldview we will discuss is how the Hebrew Bible is read in blended beliefs. By blended beliefs, I refer to people who hold worldviews that mix different aspects of the worldviews that I have covered so far.

For example, a person might be Jewish, but they also don't believe in God. This person would embrace the philosophy of naturalism, but they would also celebrate their Jewish heritage. This person would have a blended belief. Ultimately, we all have blended beliefs to one extent or another. In blended beliefs, people take different aspects of the previous worldviews that we discussed and combine them to form their individual, unique view of the Hebrew Bible.

It is important for us to recognize the deep complexities of religious belief. As I discussed in the previous chapter, this can be seen clearly in how different Christians view the Bible in different ways even though they technically profess the same faith in Jesus. Politically conservative Christians interpret the Bible very differently than liberal Christians do. Sadly, it is common for conservative and liberal Christians to accuse each other of being false versions of their faith. This type of harsh judgment is common in all factions among people. This is true within all people groups and in how they approach those outside of their groups.

Outside of Judaism and Christianity, many other religions tend to see the Old Testament as a sacred text that came from God. In Mormonism or the Church of Jesus Christ of Latter-Day Saints, the Old Testament is viewed as the first of at least three testaments. The Christian Bible is viewed as parts one and two of God's story, and the Book of Mormon is seen as the third and final revelation of God to humanity. However, Mormons would say that the King James Version of the Christian Bible is the only true version that was inspired by God. Regarding this view of the KJV Bible, there are many Christians that would agree with this idea. People who practice the faith of the Jehovah's Witnesses also believe that the Old Testament is part of their Bible. But only if it is translated in their version.

Gnosticism, which was an ancient religion that diverged from mainstream Christianity, viewed the Old Testament as the Evil Testament. In the view of Gnosticism, the New Testament was written to expose the God of the Old Testament as the devil himself. The God of the Old Testament is portrayed as evil and pathetic, while Jesus is seen as the non-human God of the New Testament. In Gnosticism, Jesus came to save people from the evil Old Testament

God. The ideas of Gnosticism are still seen in popular culture today. They can be found in Hollywood movies and sitcoms when people openly make a distinction between the Old Testament and New Testament God.

Finally, religions that many refer to as "New Age" or "Universalist" also hold to the view that the Old Testament is a sacred text. They are the ones who say that all religions of the world should coexist with each other in perfect harmony. You may have seen a bumper sticker with this image on the back of someone's car before. It combines many different popular religious symbols into the word "coexist."

Image 10: Popular "Coexist" Logo

In this worldview, all religions lead to Heaven. Going to Heaven is a universal outcome of being a good human being, and all people are naturally born good. Regardless of any faith, the Hebrew Bible has become a very influential piece of literature on the ideas of the modern Western world. As we close the first volume of this series, I invite you to examine your personal worldview. What do you believe? And why do you believe that?

My Approach in This Series

I want to make you aware of my basic worldview. This way, you will know where I stand in relationship to some of the major topics that we have discussed so far in this book. In writing this series, I intend to continue to remain flexible in my presentation of all the material. I want this series to help every student learn about the Hebrew Bible regardless of their background.

I have a unique view of the Bible that I do not have enough space to fully describe in this series. But my general approach is a combination of a Christian background with special emphasis on the Hebraic cultural and historical context in which the stories of the Bible took place. These personal views will not fully come out in my writing until Volume III of this series.

I do believe there is a God, and I believe that the Bible is His Message. I would describe the Bible as a written testimony about the Word of God. I do not believe the Word of God is a book. I believe the Word of God is a Person (John 1:1-14, John 5:39-40, & Revelation 19:11-16). I think the "Old Testament" is a terrible and insulting name for the Hebrew Bible. I only use this phrase for the sake of common identification with the text since it is the most common designation for this text in the Western world.

I am generally conservative in my view of the Hebrew Bible. This means I generally treat the stories of the whole Bible, including Genesis, as actual human history. I typically refer to the Torah as being written by Moses and many of the Psalms as written by David. But I am not dogmatic on any of these views. I like open discussions with everyone who disagrees with me. I enjoy having my views challenged by others. I see great value in reading the whole Bible with a variety of perspectives in mind. This is why I have taken such careful notes and listed the liberal and popular scholarly views of the Old Testament. I will take note of more of these scholarly interpretations of the Bible throughout this series.

I believe that Jesus of Nazareth—called Yeshua in Aramaic—is the true Messiah of the Jewish people. I believe that the Hebrew Bible anticipates Yeshua. However, I see clearly that the true heart of God is revealed just as much in the so-called "Old Testament" as it is in the New Testament. While I recognize the New Covenant as coming with Yeshua the Messiah (or Jesus Christ), I do not refer to God's former covenants with other people as "the Old Covenant." Instead, I prefer to call them the "Original Covenant."

God's covenants with His people in the Hebrew Bible are foundational for understanding what takes place in the writings of the New Covenant books. They are also foundational for understanding what will happen in the future. Just like the *Book of Revelation* in the New Testament, the books of the Prophets in the Hebrew Bible reveal vital information about the future of the world. They describe how God will restore all things and bring paradise to us in His timing. In my view, all this will be accomplished through Jesus Christ.

In the third and final volume of this series, I will discuss the narrative content of the Bible. When I do this, I will assume major themes such as God's covenants with people, the fall of humanity, God's plan of redemption, and other common Christian themes. But sometimes I discuss these themes with slightly different terminology than that which is traditional. I will emphasize the fact that God legitimately had personal relationships with many different people in the narrative of the Hebrew Bible. I will also insist that He still has legitimate, personal relationships with people who seek Him today.

If you are reading this and you have never met this God of the

Hebrew Bible, I invite you to encounter Him with me as we study His story in this series. Yahweh is not a bloodthirsty warlord. He is a compassionate Deliverer. He is not focused on sin or evil. He is focused on the goodness and the holiness that He creates and that He is. He is the Champion of the oppressed. He lifts up those who are downtrodden, and He humbles those in positions of authority who abuse others. I am convinced that this God loves you and that He died for you, and that now He lives again so that He can be with you.

The Hebrew Bible is the story of how this God made you and He wants to be with you in paradise. He wants to be where you are. He wants to bring Heaven down to Earth just as it was in the beginning in the Garden of Eden. I close this volume by quoting a powerful passage from the Hebrew Bible that comes from Joel 2:27-32. This chapter describes the day of God's great judgment on the whole world. This judgment brings destruction to those who are evil and paradise for those who are righteous. The Lord, or Yahweh, says in this passage:

> "Then you will know that I AM in Israel, that I AM YHWH your God, and that there is no other; My people will never be ashamed. And afterward, I will pour out My Spirit on all flesh. Your sons and daughters will prophesy, your old men will dream dreams, your young men will see visions. Even on My servants, both men and women, I will pour out My Spirit in those days. I will show wonders in the heavens and on the earth, blood and fire and plumes of smoke. The sun will be turned to darkness and the moon to blood before the coming of the great and dreadful Day of YHWH. And it will come to pass that whosoever will call on the Name of YHWH will be saved."

God is not far from you. He is always near, closer than your skin is to your bones. He is eager to answer you when you call. He is able to save you from every danger in this world and in the next. For all who are willing, call out to Him. Receive His Spirit. Then He will plant paradise in your heart and make it grow out all around you.

Image References

Image 1: Worldwide Religions Chart
https://cdn.wrytin.com/images/wrytup/r/1024/img-20190418-193924-jumq5fp4.jpeg

Image 2: Seeing Clearly through Glasses
https://previews.123rf.com/images/peapop/peapop0803/peapop080300011/2715003-een-bril-boven-een-boek-in-de-lenzen-is-alles-duidelijk-buiten-is-blured-noot-voor-de-inspecteurs-de.jpg

Image 3: My Glasses
Original photo, taken by the author on iPhone.

Image 4: Ugaritic Stele of El
https://emp.byui.edu/satterfieldb/ugarit/Stele%20of%20El.jpg

Image 5: Taanach Cult Stand featuring references to Yahweh & Asherah Together
http://jerusalem.nottingham.ac.uk/items/show/106

Image 6: *Kuntillet Ajrud Shrine Inscriptions* Dated Between 825 – 775 BCE
https://www.messagetoeagle.com/wp-content/uploads/2017/04/yahwehasherah.jpg

Image 7: *Khirbet el-Qom Burial Inscriptions* Dated Between 750 – 700 BCE
http://jerusalem.nottingham.ac.uk/items/show/149

Image 8: *Table of Contents in a King James Version Bible*
Original photo of a page from the author's personal Bible.

Image 9: *Table of Contents in a Tree of Life Version Bible*
Original photo of a page from the author's personal Bible.

Image 10: Popular "Coexist" Logo
https://i.kym-cdn.com/photos/images/original/001/141/805/92f.jpg

Made in the USA
Columbia, SC
22 March 2025